Interpreting th

Rev. Joanna J. Seibert MD

Interpreting the World to the Church
Volume 2

Sermons for Special Times

Blessed Hope Publishing

Impressum / Imprint

Bibliografische Information der Deutschen Nationalbibliothek: Die Deutsche Nationalbibliothek verzeichnet diese Publikation in der Deutschen Nationalbibliografie; detaillierte bibliografische Daten sind im Internet über http://dnb.d-nb.de abrufbar.

Alle in diesem Buch genannten Marken und Produktnamen unterliegen warenzeichen-, marken- oder patentrechtlichem Schutz bzw. sind Warenzeichen oder eingetragene Warenzeichen der jeweiligen Inhaber. Die Wiedergabe von Marken, Produktnamen, Gebrauchsnamen, Handelsnamen, Warenbezeichnungen u.s.w. in diesem Werk berechtigt auch ohne besondere Kennzeichnung nicht zu der Annahme, dass solche Namen im Sinne der Warenzeichen- und Markenschutzgesetzgebung als frei zu betrachten wären und daher von jedermann benutzt werden dürften.

Bibliographic information published by the Deutsche Nationalbibliothek: The Deutsche Nationalbibliothek lists this publication in the Deutsche Nationalbibliografie; detailed bibliographic data are available in the Internet at http://dnb.d-nb.de.

Any brand names and product names mentioned in this book are subject to trademark, brand or patent protection and are trademarks or registered trademarks of their respective holders. The use of brand names, product names, common names, trade names, product descriptions etc. even without a particular marking in this work is in no way to be construed to mean that such names may be regarded as unrestricted in respect of trademark and brand protection legislation and could thus be used by anyone.

Coverbild / Cover image: www.ingimage.com

Verlag / Publisher:
Blessed Hope Publishing
ist ein Imprint der / is a trademark of
OmniScriptum GmbH & Co. KG
Heinrich-Böcking-Str. 6-8, 66121 Saarbrücken, Deutschland / Germany
Email: info@blessedhope-publishing.com

Herstellung: siehe letzte Seite /
Printed at: see last page
ISBN: 978-3-639-50143-8

Interpreting the World to the Church

VOLUME 2
Sermons for Special Times

REV. JOANNA J SEIBERT, MD, DEACON

To all the Episcopal congregations and their ministers
who listened, responded, and guided me as I preached:
St. Margaret's, Trinity Cathedral, St. Luke's, St. Mark's, and Holy Spirit.

To the College of Preachers at the National Cathedral
and their teachers, where I found my voice.

CONTENTS

PREFACE

The title of this book, *Interpreting the World to the Church,* comes from the examination of a deacon in the Episcopal Church at ordination from the Book of Common Prayer (BCP).

> "As a deacon in the Church, you are to study the Holy Scriptures, to seek nourishment from them, and to model your life upon them. You are to make Christ and his redemptive love known, by your word and example, to those among whom you live, and work, and worship. You are to interpret to the Church the needs, concerns, and hopes of the world . . ."
>
> Book of Common Prayer BCP 543

Thank you for listening and making music with this deacon trying in all our ways to connect with God, staying connected and being a part of the community within and around us as well as the community beyond us, "interpreting the world to the church." It has been a privilege to spend this time with you.

Joanna

Joanna Seibert. *Photograph by Paula Volpe.*

15B Babette's Feast

John 6:53–59
Trinity Cathedral • August 20, 2006

Hallelujah! This one word is repeated over and over again by an elderly villager in Isak Dinesan's short story, "Babette's Feast." The Danish movie received the Academy Award in 1986 for Best Foreign Film. The story takes place in a remote Jutland community in western Denmark.[1,2] Babette, a refuge from the 1871 civil war in Paris arrives mysteriously one night to be the housekeeper and cook for two aging sisters, Martina and Philippa. She is sent there by Philippa's former singing coach who wanted Philippa to become an operatic star. Both pious sisters have given up their own lives and love to carry on the puritanical ministry of their deceased father in this small costal settlement.[3] Their father was the founder of a religious sect based on a return to Reformation principles. Martina was named for Martin Luther and Philippa for Luther's friend, Philip Melanchthon. As the years pass, Babette's only French connection is a lottery ticket that a relative renews for her each year. And you guessed it, after twelve years in exile she wins the French lottery, a prize of ten thousand francs. At the same time the sisters are planning a simple celebration with the remaining congregation on the hundredth anniversary of their father's birth. Babette surprises the sisters by offering to prepare "a real French dinner" for the event with some of her money. The two sisters live to serve; they are unacquainted with *being served*. The exchange between the sisters and Babette is an icon illuminating the generosity of God and our response to that generosity. The sisters reluctantly agree.

Since their charismatic father's death, the congregation has become joyless. Old quarrels and fears have resurfaced. One woman constantly nags a man about whether God will forgive them a sin of their youth. The old hymns they sing fail to bring any sense of comfort and community. The sisters' devotion is no longer appreciated. What is ultimately lacking in this remote community is grace. Their religion has become abstract and remote, a set of brittle orthodoxies rather than a lived faith.

Soon the sister's consent turns to alarm as they grasp the scope of Babette's plans when boatloads of supplies arrive from Paris, a live turtle, quail, exotic wines. As Babette begins her elaborate preparations, the sisters fear they have led their congregation to a Satanic Sabbath by a sorcerer. They meet with the group and decide they will eat the meal, but pretend they have lost their sense of taste. They will make no comment on the delicacies they have neither seen nor eaten before, pretending they are eating their usual diet of bread-mush and boiled cod.

However, Babette has become a vessel for the incarnation, for grace itself. Her meal is both a feast and a sacrifice; and, like a sacrament, it has an efficacious effect. Martina, Philippa and the others come to the elaborate dinner in their staunch plainness. The feast table is resplendent with silver candles, fancy serviettes, sparkling china. A last minute guest, General Lorens Loewenholm, is also resplendent in uniform. He tastes the first wine to be served, the Amontillado. "The finest wine I have ever tasted!" he says. Next come real turtle soup and Blinis Demidoff, thin pancakes with caviar and sour cream. At the general's astonished exclamation of "incredible!" the other diners sit quietly eating and drinking with the same blank, disinterested expressions they have had every day for thirty years. One of the women tastes the vintage champagne and innocently, wonderfully describes it as a kind of lemonade. The finest wine is poured for each course. The main course is *Cailles en sarcophages,* truffle stuffed quails in their pastry shell coffins. Hmmm. Were quail served at another feast some years earlier in another wilderness with another delicacy called manna? In typical French style the next course is salad, then cheese, cake, exotic fruit, brandy and finally coffee. Too much food for 7:30 am church!

But the meal works mysteriously on the guests in unexpected ways. Some reminisce about their absent master, making the feast a true memorial meal. But our fortuitous military guest, Lorens, Martina's former lover, perceives the meal, and the hand behind it, for what it is, just as the disciples on the Emmaus road came to recognize the Lord in the breaking of bread. As you have guessed, Babette formerly owned a famous Paris restaurant. Lorens recounts from memory only one comparable meal, years ago in Paris, prepared by someone with the "ability to transform a dinner into a love affair that makes no distinction between bodily and spiritual appetite."

As the extravagant celebration works its transformation, the polarities begin to blur; the distance between seeming opposites fades. Bitterness is replaced by sweet exchanges. Phillipa sings with an angelic voice; the company silently, peacefully, listens—feeling, remembering. Martina and Lorens gaze lovingly at each other; the two who agonized over a past elicit relationship kiss; other conflicts are touched and resolved.

The concluding highlight of the story is the General's speech. He expresses the Pastor's words spoken so long ago, illuminated now for all. "Mercy and truth, my friends, have met together. Righteousness and bliss shall kiss one another." Babette finally reveals to the sisters that she is the famous chef of the Cafe Anglais—an artist who longs to express her creative genius. She tells them that the dinner cost all of the ten thousand francs. She is now poor. The village and the people are her home forever.

Jesus says, "Unless you eat the flesh of the Son of Man and drink his blood, you have no life in you. Those who eat my flesh and drink my blood have eternal life."

Babette's Feast is a film about the opening of the hearts of a small puritanical community by a heavenly banquet. It is a cinematic icon of the Eucharist.[4] Today's gospel is about the Eucharist. It is about another feast by the one who gave all so that we too might be transformed, have new life today, the beginning of eternal life. This modern story of the Eucharist illustrates this life changing transformation, our own transfiguration that can occur when we offer and partake of this sacrificial meal of grace. This is the reason we are here today. The same joy and celebration are here. Come. The meal us offered. Let us partake of the feast.

1. Valerie O'Connell, *Babette's Feast*, a review, John Mark Ministries, December 11, 2003.
2. David O'Connor, *Babette's Feast* Summary, OpenCourseWare, University of Notre Dame, 2012.
3. Steven D. Greydanus, *Babette's Feast*, Vatican film list, 1987.
4. Robert A. Flanagan, *Babette's Feast: The Generosity of God,* Jacob's Well, Spring/Summer, 1998.

16B First Day Back

John 6:60–69
August 27, 2006 • Trinity Cathedral

Matthew, Mark, and Luke, the synoptic gospels, describe in detail the scene and setting of the first Lord's Supper, but it is this gospel of John which tells us the effect, the consequences of the Eucharist in our lives.[1]

"I am the bread which came down from heaven."

Sadness spills out of every pore of her body. It is our resident's first day back at work after her father's death. Yvonne has just returned from her parent's home in Texas late the night before. She and her father were very close. He also was a radiologist and her life long role model. She can barely speak she is so fragile. Almost inaudibly she says, "I thought I could do this, but I don't see how I can make it through this day." We sit down in front of viewing boxes of X-rays. But instead of reading the films in front of us, we talk about her father, she cries, and then we seek distraction in our work. We talk again, she cries, and then we read more x-rays together.

Memories flood through my own mind of the first days after my father died over fifteen years earlier. I remember how I wanted to say to each person I met, "Did you know that my father has died?" It was too hard to comprehend that the world could keep going on, business as usual when I had just lost my father.

"The one who eats this bread will live forever."

The most significant person in my growing up years was my Baptist grandfather. When he died over twenty years ago I was devastated almost as much as Yvonne is now. I think back and try to recall, "What helped me the most get through that sadness and loss?" I remember that I was moved to do something to honor my grandfather and his life. I was a heavy smoker. I mean 20 pack years. I can still see my grandfather's loving eyes and hear his deep voice, "I wish so much that you did not smoke." I had tried to stop many times but never was able to do so. I knew my quitting smoking would please my grandfather. By some miracle, I was given that grace and have not smoked a cigarette since December 7, 1979, the day of his funeral. It was a miracle, a real spiritual healing. My grandfather not only showed me unconditional love in its truest form while he lived, but now even in death is still caring for me by literally saving my life.

The spirit of my grandfather gave me the strength to do something I had never been able to do before. Those who have died, those in eternal life, are constantly with us in spirit to comfort and guide and love us as much and maybe sometimes even more than when they were living.

I think of Leigh Ann Bennett, now a practicing psychiatrist in Little Rock. Seven and 1/2 years ago when she was a resident, her father, also a radiologist, tragically committed suicide. Leigh Ann worked through her own grief by helping to spear head a foundation to educate people, especially in White County, about depression and its signs and symptoms. She was honored by our medical school with the Joycelyn Elders award for community service.

"I am the bread which came down from heaven."

I shared some of these stories with Yvonne. She, too, has already thought of honoring her father. Her eyes brighten, color returns to her face as she tells me, "My father took the Eucharist to patients in a nursing home in my home town in Texas every Saturday on his day off. He took out the sacraments the day before he died. I have this strong desire to continue his Eucharistic ministry either there or here in Little Rock."

"This is the bread that came down from heaven . . . the one who eats this bread will live forever."

Suddenly memories of my mother's death just one year earlier flood through my consciousness. I wanted to take Eucharist to my mother in the hospital, but did not make it home in time. I then remember the day I returned to Little Rock after my mother's funeral. A friend calls, "Can you bring eucharist to the hospital on Sunday to my mother? By some miracle she is beginning to recover from a near fatal illness." Later at her mother's bedside I am strangely warmed as I observe a physical resemblance between by friend's mother and my own. I am reminded of how God often comforts us by allowing us to serve other loved ones when we can not, for unknown reasons, be with our most immediate loved ones.

"The one who eats this bread will live forever."

Later in the afternoon that day at Children's Hospital, Yvonne and I go to the neonatal intensive care nursery to evaluate a very sick newborn. As we start to perform our examination we realize that the mother who is at the bedside is Mexican and cannot speak or understand English. She has been at her baby's side all day not knowing what is going on with her very ill one-day-old son. Yvonne looks into the frightened and confused eyes of this mother and whispers, "*Yo hablo Espanol.*" Our resident speaks fluent Spanish because she is from south Texas and because her father was an immigrant from Spain. "*Su hijo esta' muy enfermo.*" She then tenderly begins to interpret our findings, explaining exactly what we are doing and describing to that young mother the serious condition of her beloved infant.

As our day together ends we both reflect through red eyes and cracking voices, "This has been a very difficult day, but how AMAZING it is how God reaches out to comfort our pain in places and through people we least expect."

This is the wisdom we are taught in the "synagogue" of a Children's Hospital. The death of someone we love is not a period at the end of a sentence, but more like a comma, where the one we love is not only in a new relationship with God but also in a new love relationship with us as well."

This day we see Christ reaching out to heal the two of us from our losses, recent and past. God uses a young physician in great emotional pain that still is able to reach out to a young mother also in great distress. They both most probably may never meet again, but they have a glimpse of the Christ, *el Christo,* abiding in each other. They have a glimpse of the shape of each other's heart.

All three of us are feed eucharist by a community of ancestors, loved ones, with whom in our past we ate the bread of heaven, and now THEY live with Christ, and with us forever.

This should be the end of this story, but there is a postscript. I sent an email to Yvonne asking permission to tell her story. This is her reply:

"I remember this day as if it were yesterday, though two and a half years have passed, and with time and prayer, healing.

One of the things you told me that day was that I would think of and feel the presence my dad more now that he is gone, than had he been physically present. How true that is! No emotion is spared thoughts of him — happy, sad, anxious . . . One occasion in particular I wanted to share with you the day it happened, but, despite good intentions, offered up a prayer rather than a phone call. Now you have given me the opportunity to share it.

On my birthday this past year, I woke up, of course, with thoughts of my dad. I went to church. On my way out I heard the hurried footsteps of Sr. Dorothy, a nun/nurse with whom I had become friends through my persistence in trying to get involved with this local church. Would you believe, she asked me if I would be interested in becoming a Eucharistic minister! On my birthday! What a gift! I walked home with my emotions 180 degrees turned from what they had been, filled with peace and joy and undeniably feeling the presence of God right in step with me. Never abandoned!! Thanks for my Dad! Thanks be to God!"

"The one who eats this bread will live forever."

1. Raymond Brown, *The Gospel According to John,* p. 292.

INTERPRETING SAINTS

All Saints B Death of Our Brother Lazarus
John 11:32–44

Martha said to Jesus, "Lord, if you had been here, my brother would not have died."

And just a little later, Mary's first words to Jesus are the same as her sister's, "Lord, if you had been here, my brother would not have died."

My brother died last year on Boxing Day, the second day of Christmas. He died less than four months after his 70th birthday, almost exactly the same age as our father when he died. My brother was born on Labor Day and died on Boxing Day. We will have to work on the significance of all that. Boxing Day is traditionally the day after Christmas when servants in English households receive a gift from their employer in a "box", and of course Labor Day honors those who are working and gives them an extra day of rest. I do know Jim loved Christmas. My brother also died on the day our church calendar honors Stephen, the first deacon and martyr. I don't know about a martyr, but my brother was definitely a survivor. He had open-heart surgery, three cancers and at least three strokes. I did something I have never done before shortly after my brother died. I prayed asking him what he would like for us to say about him. I have given homilies at many funerals but never have prayed that question to the person who has died. I now wish I had. This is what immediately came to me that my brother said: "I tried to be a good man, and I loved my family." "I tried to be a good man, and I loved my family." So that was my message from my brother. I know he dearly loved his family and was very proud of each of his sons. He loved his community, serving so faithfully as a banker, a member of the Boys and Girls Club and the school board. I know he especially loved his church where he also served so faithfully. Since the Episcopal Church is a love we both shared, we talked about it often. Only once did we have the privilege of serving at an altar together. That was at our mother's funeral where we both were Eucharistic ministers serving the chalice. My brother was an eight o'clock churchgoer. They are a different breed, a little more private, a little quieter, sometimes a little more conservative. They get the ear of the rector after the service, as there are so few people present that early. My brother loved serving on the vestry, another rare breed. If an eight o'clocker is a lector or Eucharistic minister, they serve more often than those at the later service as my brother did. I tried to talk my brother into becoming a deacon, which I think could have happened if he had had a little more time. The church is in the genes of our family. It comes out in so many different forms, but we cannot escape it.

My brother was a believer and there is no doubt that he now lives in the resurrection, just as he experienced so many resurrections in this life. What is life like in the resurrection? I have no idea and I have learned to beware of people who tell us what it is like. I always wish that our friend Lazarus had recorded what life after death was for him, but many describe Lazarus' experience as resuscitation rather than a resurrection. Our only real model is Jesus. After the resurrection Jesus is the same and different. He walks through locked doors but still eats fish. He still has his wounds on his feet and hands and side, but they are healing enough so that he can walk. He suddenly appears and then without notice disappears as he did on the road to Emmaus. Sometimes people who know Jesus so well like Mary Magdalene do not recognize him at first.

We can only imagine what this new life is like for my brother and all our loved ones who have died. Our daughter, Joanna, sent me a text when she heard my brother had died saying she was cleaning her house and crying and listening to Elvis music. Yes, I know my brother was overcome by meeting Jesus face to face, but I have no doubt that his next words were asking Jesus about "The King." Our family will always remember hearing my brother singing Elvis' favorites at Karaoke. A secret that few know is that as a child he was a boy soprano and sang solos in churches especially at Christmas. He sang the Italian Christmas Carol, *Gesu Bambino,* the best.

I imagine that my brother's body is restored and renewed and he is again strong and that he is that jovial, good-humored positive self again, just waiting to help someone else out. If there are cars or silver or shoes in the resurrected life, I know he is polishing them. If there is a wide screen TV in the resurrected life, I know my brother will be there watching golf or football or basketball or better yet he now may be able to get the best seats and to go to every NC State game, but I am wondering if they allow you to wear red in the life after death.

People often ask how to work through the death of someone you love. My experience from Walking the Mourner's Path is to do something to honor their life and your relationship with them. The brother I want to remember is the one who loved life and enjoyed life and loved serving others. Perhaps that is what I want to remember, to love life and enjoy each moment and serve others. This is a gift; it was his gift. I will always especially remember that my brother was the only one present with our mother when she died. He also cared for our Aunt Rosie until she was in her 90's. That was servant ministry. Perhaps in some way I will honor my brother by serving others, and also remembering to love life.

My image of the resurrected life is that the people there who love us are constantly praying for us. Also those in the resurrection can now be with us always, as before when they were alive, they were only with us when they were physically present. The God of my understanding does not give us a relationship with someone who cares about us and loves us and then abruptly stops it. The death of someone you love is not like a period at the end of a sentence but more like a comma, where the relationship continues but in a different way. I know our parents and our grandparents so loved my brother. I am sometimes more acutely aware of the presence of my grandparents, my husband's parents, almost like angels keeping me from harm and allowing me to do things I know I would not be able to do for myself. Be aware that you too may feel your loved one's prayers and their presence and their love even more than you knew when they were alive with you. My prayer on this All Saints is that we will all keep and hold on to all the memories of those we loved and honor their presence and what we learned from them.

All Saints. 50th year remembrance of integration of Central High School Little Rock, Arkansas

Holy Spirit, Gulfshores, Alabama • November 4, 2007

"Let us now sing the praises of famous men . . . and women . . . our ancestors in their generation."

All Saints is our church's family reunion day. It is the day we pull out our family photograph album and remember where we came from.[1]

"I looked and there was a great multitude that no one could count."

But when we look closer at the individual portfolios of the saints, we notice that they were not, well, "saints." They were ordinary people with the same doubts and fears as the rest of us.

In Little Rock last month we commemorated the 50th anniversary of the integration of Central High School in 1957. Trinity Cathedral partnered with a nearby black church Bethel AME planning two services to remember what the church did and did not do during that crisis and joining together to make a new start. Our congregations learned much about each other and our past.

In 1957, the parents of the nine black students who tried to enter Central High could not accompany them, but their ministers could. A call went out to black and white ministers to walk with the students. Only two white ministers responded. One was a Presbyterian minister, Dunbar Ogden. His son has written a book about his father's experience called, *My Father Said Yes.* This is how Rev. Ogden describes that morning he first met the students:

> I can't say the children looked afraid. The word I would use to describe them is thoughtful. They looked just like any eight boys and girls of high school age, fine clean-cut, youngsters. I had an impulse to throw my arms around them and I thought: they're so much like the young people in my church, so much like the young people in my home.
>
> One of the Negro men came over to me and said, "Well, Reverend Ogden, are you going with us?' And I said, 'Well, I don't know." And

he said, "Well, you know at 8:10 we're going to start walking." And everyone was silent.

And I thought something should be said, being a minister, I guess. I didn't actually offer a prayer but I said, "Now, young people, you are doing something this morning that takes a lot of faith and courage. We don't know what that mob is going to try to do to you. But we know it is a very bad situation. I want you to remember your own Martin Luther King and what he said about non-violence. There was a man named Gandhi in India and he had the same idea and he helped to win the freedom of his people. Of course there was one whom we call Jesus Christ and it is written that when he was reviled, he reviled not again."

And about this time, a Negro came over and said, "It's 8:09 now. Are you going with us or not?"

I said, "I don't know."

And he said, "Reverend Ogden, isn't it about time you make up your mind?"

And then, I can say more in retrospect, this had the effect of making me feel yes, I had to make up my mind whether I was going all the way.

And then I had a very strange feeling, that we describe as something of a prophetic experience. I had the strange feeling, as clear as day, and I felt this is right; this is what I should do.

There was not the slightest doubt but that I should do it. I ought to do it. And I felt this was the will of God for me, every bit of fear just drained out.

"All right," my father said. "I will go with you." [2]

In that moment he makes a choice that will change his life, and the course of history. He turns and begins to walk down Park Street toward Central High. He does not look back. Shortly afterwards, Rev. Ogden is asked by his congregation to leave Little Rock.

"Their bodies are buried in peace, but their names live on generation after generation."

Let me tell you about two other men who were short on height but long on love of the Lord. One is dead and one is still alive.

The living saint is Bishop Desmond Tutu who chaired the Truth and Reconciliation Commission in South Africa, which heard grievances from those who suffered during the apartheid era. His daughter, Naomi, preached at Trinity commemorating the integration of Central High School. The commission gave voice to stories in the hope of burying past bitterness. This is an excerpt from one of his addresses. "People may commit demonic acts but they are not demons. It is very dangerous to demonize our opponents. Everyone has the potential of becoming a saint."

"Who are those robed in white and where have they come from?"

These passages from Revelation are very important to Archbishop Tutu.[3] To him this book of Revelation is poetry and liturgy. It is not a Rand-McNally map of heaven. It is not a timetable for the end of the world. It is full of encouragement, hope and comfort, especially for the oppressed. When Tutu was fighting against apartheid, he would say, "DON'T GIVE UP! DON'T GET DISCOURAGED! I HAVE READ THE END OF THE BOOK! WE WIN!"

"There were those who led the people by their counsels and by their knowledge of the people's lore."

Where were you the night of April 4, 1968? My husband and I were seniors in medical school in Memphis. That night Martin Luther King was assassinated outside of the Loraine Motel.[3] Memphis became a police state. Clergy in Memphis decided to respond by marching to the office of the mayor, Henry Loeb. The ministers gathered at St. Mary's Episcopal Cathedral. At the last moment, the Dean, William Dimmick, who later became the bishop of Michigan, (also baptized our two sons) went into the Cathedral and took the cross from the high altar. Holding it high above him (he was a very short man), he led the march down Poplar Avenue to City Hall.

"I saw another angel ascending from the rising of the sun . . . saying do not damage the earth or the sea or the trees."

The air was electric. Down the streets they marched. One Methodist minister writes[4] about one moment he will never forget. As the clergy are marching down Poplar Avenue, up ahead, he sees an elderly woman sitting on her front porch. As the procession approaches her, she stands up and screams, "GET THAT CROSS BACK IN THE CHURCH WHERE IT BELONGS!" I have left a picture of Dean Dimmick at the mayor's office in the fellowship hall. He took the cross out of the cathedral into the streets of a city on the verge of riot. He taught us where Christ was that day. Christ was out walking the streets of Memphis. Today my prayer is that at the end of this service we will remember Dean Dimmick's example and symbolically carry your processional cross out side this building into the streets of this city and this state.

"Who are these, robed in white, and where have they come from?"

On All Saints we worship amidst a great fluttering of wings, the whole host of heaven crowding the air above our heads. The old saints in their white robes and the baby saints in their diapers, passing one another on their way in and out of this world. Can you feel what a crowd we are today? Matthew is there, Thomas, Dunbar, William, Stephen, and Mary, plus all those whom we have loved and lost during the past year. We will soon call their names during the prayers. Listen for them to answer, "PRESENT."

On All Saints Day we make the very bold claim that all these people are our relatives.[4] They belong to us and we to them. Because of them and because of one another and because of the God who binds us all together, we can do more than any of us had dreamed to do alone. We do not have to do this alone. We have this company of saints sitting right here whom we can see plus those we cannot see—all egging us on, calling our names and shouting themselves hoarse with encouragement to us. We are a part of them and they are a part of us and all of us are knit together in this communion of saints.

"Their offspring will continue forever, and their glory will never be blotted out.

Their bodies are buried in peace, but their name lives on generation after generation."

1. Barbara Brown Taylor, "God's Handkerchiefs," *Home by Another Way,* pp 208–212.
2. Dunbar H. Ogden, *My Father Said Yes: A White Pastor in Little Rock School Integration,* pp. 26–27.
3. Flemming Rutledge, "Apocryphal or Real?", *The Bible and the New York Times,* p.17.
4. Katherine Moorehead, "Stepping out of the Tent," *Preaching through the Year of Mark,* p. 75.

St. Margaret's Day
Dinner with St. Margaret

Matthew 13:44–52
St. Margaret's Episcopal Church Little Rock
November 16, 2003

I suspect that I may not be the only one who plans imaginary dinner parties.[1] If I'm day dreaming in my favorite chair on a Sunday afternoon or bored to tears at some interminable meeting, I occasionally amuse myself by planning the menu, flowers, and list of guests for a fantasy meal. Ordinary constraints do not apply. I can invite anyone I wish, living or dead.

Today the guest of honor is Margaret, Queen of Scotland. Some of you may know her well. She visits this church often, in fact she was just here two weeks ago on All Saints Sunday to help launch our capital campaign; but you can always count on her to appear on this her name day.

I have never really dined with a queen before. I am more nervous than usual about today's dinner party for Margaret, for she is highly cultured. She introduced spiced meat, French wines, and table manners to the court in Scotland. I think I may invite Richard Schreiber and Jay Bruno to help me and also be guests. They know a great deal about French wines. I think Kay and Richard Arnold have been to some state dinners, so I will invite them as well and see if they can advise us on the table settings.

I'm not quite certain how to address our guest of honor. Should I say Princess Margaret? Margaret is a Saxon princess born in Hungry where her father had been in exile since he was an infant. Her grandfather is Edmund Ironsides, King of England.[2, 3] Margaret returns to the English court when she is 10 years old, but flees again when she is 20 in 1066 when William the Conqueror invades England. She seeks refuge in Scotland where she is courted by King Malcolm and marries him four years later to become his queen. So probably I should address her as your majesty.

Oh, goodness, there she is! She is so much shorter and thinner than I thought she would be."Your majesty, how thrilled we are that you have come today."

I hope she notices we have put out our best linens and embroidery and are wearing some of our finest vestments, for you know she started a sewing guild for the women at the Scottish court to provide elegant vestments and linens for the church in Scotland.

"Queen Margaret, how honored we are that you have allowed us to name this church for you and how excited we are that you have come to dine with us today. I know you have a very busy schedule and that intercontinental traveling is so much more difficult these days."

"Bless all of you. It is my privilege to be with you. Don't go to any trouble. You know I am 957 years old and really don't require as much maintenance as I used to. Now I will expect from you a much bigger dinner party in 43 years in the year 2046 when I celebrate my 1000th birthday. I am counting on you to make that a very special occasion, but today, just keep it simple."

"Queen Margaret, I want to introduce you to some other guests, Kay, Richard, Jay, and Richard. I also thought you might like to dine with some other saints who have churches named after them here in the Little Rock area. Over there trying out the Scottish haggis are Mark, Luke, Matthew, and Michael. They are much older than you, but I know you like older men."

She had a twinkle in her eye. "You are so right. My husband Malcolm is more than 15 years older than I am. However, I also know these four gentlemen you are referring to very well."

I suddenly realize that in Christ's body there are no strangers. Church history is holographic, just like Scripture. We can enter it from any angle, and we all are there, in Christ. When we have conversation with or read about the lives of the saints we slightly shift our famous three-legged stool to put tradition front and center, though the weight is still equally supported by Scripture and by reason.

"Can you tell us a little about how you became so admired after you a Englishwoman became Queen of Scotland in 1070?"

"Well, you know my predecessor as Queen of Scotland was Lady Macbeth. Poor thing. It was terrible. Her husband killed Duncan who was Malcolm's father. So when I became queen, the people were very ready for change."

"Why do you think this gospel reading about giving up all that we have for a pearl of great price has been chosen for your name day?"

"This parable has been so true in my own life. When my mother and my sister and brother and I fled England after the Norman conquest, I had planned to return to Hungry to my mother's home, but a fierce gale drove us northwards where we were guests of the Bishop of Durham and then we sailed up the coast and landed in Scotland where we were met by Malcolm. I knew Malcolm in the English court when he fled there after his father was killed. I never wanted to marry and really wanted to become a nun.[3] I am what you might describe as a Benedictine contemplative. However, Malcolm courted me for four years, and finally I gave in and I never regretted it. My relationship with God was that pearl of great price, but I found it in a different field that I thought I would originally travel to. The field in which I found the pearl was in servant ministry to my family and my new country INSTEAD OF IN A CONVENT."

"Queen Margaret, I guess you realize that you stand alone as a saint canonized as a mother of eight children who died surrounded by her children. The other women saints are virgins or widows."

At our table the candles sputter. I detect tears welling in Margaret's eyes. "Well, you know I was a widow for a few days before I died. My dear husband and oldest son were killed treacherously four days before my own death in my 47th year. I am so proud of my children and my grandchildren. You know three of my sons became kings of Scotland and my daughter and my granddaughter were queens of England. My son, King David, was also made a saint."

Matthew then comes and sits beside us and puts his hand on Margaret's shoulder. "Margaret," he says, "I have always wanted to tell you how honored I am that the passage from my book about the pearl of great price was chosen for your saint day."

Margaret's countenance changes back to her composed self. "Yes, I like it as well. YOU know my name, Margaret, comes from the Greek word Margaron that means pearl. I am named for Saint Margaret of Antioch who was martyred in 4th century Turkey. Now there's an interesting woman."

"Queen Margaret, how would you contrast our church today with yours in the 11th century?"

"Dear ones, there are so many similarities. We also struggled as you do with theological and liturgical differences. Ours was a struggle between the Celtic and the Roman views of God. Finally after a millennium you seem to be honoring both. I would encourage you to see and honor the God in each other a little sooner than in a 1000 years."

"Queen Margaret, tell us how to keep our faith, keep our courage, and find that pearl of great price that you seem to have found."

"Each of us will find the kingdom and its treasure on a little different path, hidden in a little different field, on a slightly different sea. For me, I find my faith by being constantly reminded of the presence of God in my life by daily prayer, meditation, scripture reading, and the Eucharist, which I helped institute more often in Scotland. I also openly share with others my faith, whatever pearls I have found. You know my husband still cannot read, so I often read scripture or prayers to him.

I also found the kingdom, the presence of Christ, so thinly disguised in the poor of my country. Our family ate with and met with and opened our home daily to the poor, especially to orphans and children.[4] That is where I found Christ living most clearly in the world. If you don't know that, go there and see for yourself this hidden treasure. Look into people and places the way Jesus looked at them, and you won't miss seeing his reflection."

Margaret then rises and we all instinctively and respectfully follow her lead. "Well, this has been so enjoyable," she says. "I hope you will invite me back for dinner again soon. Next time, could you also invite Paul? I have a few things I would like to say to him about the role of women and some other matters. Bless you all."

Now in my reverie, I clear the table, put our best china in the dishwasher, and blow out the candles. The party is over. NO, that's not right. The party has just begun, again, one more time, and it will never end until the Kingdom comes. Margaret and Matthew and Luke and Michael and Mark and you and I and all the others in that great cloud of witnesses come together around Margaret's earthly table, where CHRIST JESUS is our heavenly host, and WE are now the honored guests. Bound by the Spirit, may we now take our places beside Margaret. May we be given her zeal for Christ's church and her love for Christ's people, and may we be fruitful as she was in good works. We offer thanks to God for her life and for this life of grace to which we all are called, so that here at St. Margaret's all of us may help each other find that pearl of great price.

---

1. Anne Barlett, "Taking our Places at the Table," *Sermons That Work, Preaching Through Holy Days and Holidays,* pp.143–147.

2. James Kiefer's Christian Biographies, elvis.rowan.edu.

3. Alan J. Wilson, *St. Margaret Queen of Scotland,* pp.19–29, 73 65.

4. *Lives of the Scottish Saints,* translated by WM Metcalfe, p. 61.

LENT 1A *Paul, Romans, and St. Margaret's*

Romans 5:12–19, (20–21)
February 13, 2005, on leaving St. Margaret's

A Letter from Paul to the Romans and to St. Margaret's on the first Sunday in Lent.

I, Paul, a servant of Jesus Christ, to all God's beloved in Rome and to St. Margaret's in Little Rock who are all called to be saints: Grace to you and peace from God our Father and the Lord Jesus Christ.

First I thank my God through Jesus Christ for all of you, because your faith is proclaimed throughout the world. Without ceasing I remember you always in my prayers, asking that by God's will I may somehow at last succeed in coming to you. For I am longing to see you so that I may share with you some spiritual gift to strengthen you—or rather so that we may be mutually encouraged by each other's faith.

My previous missionary journeys that you have read about encompassed over 10,000 miles.[1] I concentrated my ministry then on the eastern side of the Mediterranean, from Jerusalem to present day Turkey, Albania, Croatia, Bosnia, Serbia, and Greece. Goodness knows I need to go back there today, but I am going to leave that to you. I want to move westward, to Rome, Spain and more.

Like the church I wrote to in the capital city of Rome, I have never visited St. Margaret's in the capital city of Arkansas, but I have some very definite ideas about how you should function and I would like to share this with you, especially as you begin this Lenten season. I will try not to make this as long as my letter to the Romans. I know you have already read my letter to the Romans, and that parts of it will be read 25 times in your lectionary this year, so I do not plan to repeat many things to you today. As you know I do not write my letters personally. I have a scribe to whom I dictate. Today I am using Tertius who was also my scribe for Romans. The deacon, Phoebe, carried my letter to Rome. I am sending this letter to St. Margaret's by Canon Bosmyer. She has spent a great deal of time with me and can explain passages with which you may have difficulty. Greet her warmly. She will from time to time read my letters to you on upcoming Sundays. Perhaps there are other congregations in Little Rock who may sometimes also like to hear my letters to St. Margaret's. If the crowd becomes too large, I hear that for special occasions you often have put up a tent. This would definitely please me since you know my day job is tent making.

I have read much about your church and its members. You know I am primarily a church planter and I was so excited to hear about your congregation which was so carefully planted and planned by Canon Keller and Archdeacon Millwee. I send specific greetings to you from Archdeacon Millwee who is now with me and keeps sending me articles from the National Review and articles about you that he wants me to read.

I do see so many similarities between your church at St. Margaret's and that in Rome. You both started out with only a few members of the mother faith. In Rome the church started with Jewish Christians. At St. Margaret's there were many cradle or long time Episcopalians in the founding group. When the Jews were expelled from Rome in 49 CE by Emperor Claudius because of riots about Christ, the Gentiles became the predominate Christians in the Roman church. Today I see St. Margaret's as now made up of so many who come from other faith groups. When Nero came to power in Rome in 54 CE, the Christian Jews returned to Rome to find their church now led by Gentiles. The church in Rome had considerable conflict in beliefs between Christians of Gentile and Christians of Jewish background. I commend you that you seem to have very little conflict between members of this church from different religious backgrounds. I hope it stays that way.

If I could summarize all my letters, my entire ministry, what I would wish on my tombstone, I would say I have spent my career working for church unity and raising funds for the poor. Again, I employ you to follow my example.

Today in your lectionary you hear a small part from my letter to the Romans. It is hard to understand this letter without reading it all the way through. It is a continuous story. When you hear little snippets each Sunday, I fear you may miss what I am trying to say. I encourage you to read it as you would a letter, all at one sitting.

In regards to today's specific reading, I am talking about sin, the law, and grace, a subject of course appropriate for the first Sunday in Lent. I want you to concentrate on loving one another rather than on naming each other's sins. The commandments, the laws make Sin evident. They do not provide an escape from sin. The law cannot control sin. It only counts it.

I think you will better understand these verses if I go back and summarize why I initially wrote my letter to the Romans and comment on some similarities I see in your church. Since I am so much older than you in time, I will use some of Kathy Grieb's interpretation of my letter to speak to you in more modern terms.[1]

First I write to introduce my theology. I think I have so often received some bad press. I am looking for some better airtime. I wanted Rome and also you to hear my exact words. You may not realize what an impact that letter I wrote to the Romans has had when people down through our church's history were able to grasp what I was trying to say. A passage from Romans was instrumental in the conversion of Augustine (13:13–14.)

The commentaries of Luther and Calvin on Romans helped shape the Protestant Reformation. Unfortunately people seem continually to have difficultly understanding me. They have to read COMMENTARIES. John Wesley's heart was "strangely warmed" and his conversion occurred on Aldersgate while hearing someone read the *Preface* to Luther's commentary to Romans. Some say that hardly any book in the Bible has had the influence that my letter to the Romans has had on the church, but I will leave that conclusion to you.

I write to the Romans and I write to you to correct misunderstandings about what I teach. I have been criticized as being disloyal to Judaism.

I have sometimes been called God's defense attorney. I write to reassure Jewish Christians in Rome that God still honors his covenant with them.

But . . . I write to Gentile Christians in Rome that they also are included in God's covenant.

I also write to urge Roman Christians to quit fighting over nonessential matters and live together as a UNITY with DIVERSITY. This is the major message I now want to leave with you at St. Margaret's and the Episcopal Church at large. You must welcome those with whom you disagree. This is not optional. (Romans 14:3, 15:7, 5:10)

I write to Rome to recommend Phoebe, who is considered the first female deacon and my coworker who brought my letter to them. I also write to recommend to you the faithful deacon at this church, Cindy Fribourgh.

I write to the house churches in Rome to start building a base for operations in Spain. I also write today to you to consider becoming a base for other house churches in Little Rock. I know that is a dream of Canon Campbell and I write to ask you to support him in this.

Finally I write to proclaim the gospel of God to Rome and now to you. I am the apostle to the Gentiles, which I believe includes every one of you. I write to tell you of the righteousness of God made evident in the faithfulness of Jesus

Christ, which has changed everything forever. Nothing in all creation can separate you and me from that love of God in Christ Jesus. (8:39)

"Who will separate us from the love of Christ? Will hardship, distress, persecution, famine, nakedness, peril, or sword?

No . . . for I am convinced that neither death, nor life, nor angels, nor rulers, nor things present, nor things to come, nor powers nor height, nor depth, nor anything else in all creation, will be able to separate you and me from the love of God in Christ Jesus our Lord." (8:35–39)

Does that mean the same thing to you today as it did when I said it to the Romans almost 200 centuries ago? You can bet your life on it!! It is what you claim every time you come together here. It is why you stand and sit and kneel at this place. It is the claim you wrap yourself and each of your tiny infants in as you emerges from the baptismal font, and it will be the first thing proclaimed at your burial. I know you identify with this. I know everyone of you has had experiences in your life that were overwhelming, but somehow the love of Christ came to you, in prayers and in other members of this community gathered here.

By now you may be getting tired of hearing my story. It is time to hear your story, your letter. I appeal to you brothers and sisters. It is time for you to share your stories with one another. I am putting down my pen and asking you to write your own letter about the love of God in Christ Jesus in your life and share it with each other.

Do you have fears about doing this? Let me close with the words I sent to Nelson Mandela, another fellow prisoner, which he never used in his presidential inauguration speech in 1994, but is attributed to him:[2]

> Our deepest fear is not that we are inadequate.
> Our deepest fear is that
> we are powerful beyond measure.
> It is our light, not our darkness,
> that most frightens us.
>
> We ask ourselves:
> Who am I to be brilliant, gorgeous,
> talented, fabulous?
> Actually, who are you not to be?

You are a child of God.
Your playing small does not serve the world.
There is nothing enlightened about shrinking
so that other people will feel secure around you.

We were born to make manifest
the glory of God that is within us.
It is not just in some of us; it is in everyone.

And as we let our own light shine,
We unconsciously give other people permission to do the same.

As we are liberated from our own fear,
Our presence automatically liberates others."

And so during this Lenten season, make ready your guest room, for I, Paul, plan to spend a lot of time with you this year.

To the only wise God be glory for evermore through Jesus Christ! Amen.

1. Katherine Grieb, *The Story of Romans,* Westminister, Louisville, 2002.
2. Marianne Williamson, *A Return to Love, Reflections on the Principles of a Course in Miracles,* pp. 190–191. 1992.

INTERPRETING WEDDINGS

Marriage of Vickie and Carl Becker

November 5, 2005

"Blessed are the merciful, for they will receive mercy.

"Blessed are the pure in heart, for they will see God.

"Blessed are the peacemakers, for they will be called children of God."

Vickie, Carl, you have chosen for your gospel reading for this service, the beatitudes. I wonder if you know this will also be the gospel reading tomorrow for All Saints Sunday. Perhaps you already know that in order to stay true to all your marriage vows, you will have to become a saint. . or maybe you realize that in keeping these vows you will need the prayers and support of all the saints.

"Blessed are the poor in spirit, for theirs is the kingdom of heaven.

"Blessed are those who mourn, for they will be comforted.

I dare say that each of you here knows how Vickie and Carl met. It was on September 11, 2001. They were at a meeting in Chicago. After the disastrous plane crashes of that day, their meeting was canceled and they had nothing to do for the next several days except to get to know each other better . . . and of course the rest of the story of our country as well as Vickie and Carl's story is history. To most of us, Carl and Vickie will be living proof of how our God works resurrection out of suffering, changes curses into blessings.

I know that you are familiar with our Lord's first miracle, turning water into wine when the celebration wine ran out at a marriage feast in Cana. Turning water into a new kind of wine. . that's what happened in Chicago to Vickie and Carl on that fateful 9 /11.

I know most of you know that this is a blessing of this marriage. Vickie and Carl were indeed married almost two months ago in California on guess what date . . . September 11th.

I hope that when each of us sees you, Vickie and Carl, your presence and your love will be icons for us of resurrection out of death, turning water into new wine. And may this also be a constant reminder to the two of you, your meeting, your wedding date. . of how the God of your understanding will always do this in each part of your life, but for the two of you, especially in your married life. . bring resurrection out of great difficulties, change water into wine, change difficult times into times of blessings.

I want to remind you of one more part of the story of the wedding at Cana. Both of you are not the age of the usual couple who comes before this altar for blessings of marriage. Do you remember what the wine steward said to Jesus when he tasted the new wine at Cana? This is the best wine. Most people serve their best wine first. But you have served your best wine last. Remember this. A second part of the miracle of your marriage. God has given to the both of you the best part now later in life, the best part last. May God continue to bless you in your new life as you have blessed the lives of all of us here with your presence and your love.

"Blessed are the pure in heart, for they will see God."

INTERPRETING FUNERALS

Funeral Arthurine Harrison, former headmaster of The Cathedral School for children

Romans 8:14–19,34–35,37–39
Trinity Cathedral Little Rock • Wednesday November 10, 2010

Our dear friend Arthurine Harrison died early Sunday morning as this cathedral was preparing for All Saints services. Her name was read with the saints as we sang two of the hymns we are singing today, but I can imagine that when our witty friend heard her name read Sunday for the first time, she might have quoted another religious activist, Dorothy Day, saying, " Don't call me a saint. I do not want to be dismissed so easily."

"I sing a song of the saints of God . . . They lived not only in ages past, there are hundreds of thousands still . . . You can meet them at school, or in lanes or at sea, in church or in trains or in shops or at tea."[1]

Arthurine came to the Cathedral School in 1970 to teach the fourth grade. Her daughter Rhonda was in the first grade. Think back. I dare say most of you can remember your first and fourth grade teachers. Three years later, Rhonda was a little apprehensive about now having her mother as her fourth grade teacher, but Dean Higgins alleviated her anxiety by appointing Arthurine the principal or head master of The Cathedral School, and Arthurine or "Mrs. Harrison" as she is better known by her students, led this school to great heights for 16 more years. She was so beloved that the school office, Harrison House, was named for her. I was so impressed during Arthurine's recent hospitalizations at UAMS that so many of her former students from 20 years ago flocked to visit her, many of them in the medical profession at UAMS. It was a reminder to us all of the enormous impact that gifted grade school teachers make in our lives when we are young and as we grow older. This tribute continues as The Cathedral School choristers honor Arthurine, and the teachers of the school have prepared the reception that you are invited to after this service in Morrison Hall.

It is hard to believe, but Arthurine has not always been an Episcopalian. She grew up Southern Baptist and like many of us became Methodists, but it was her daughter, Rhonda, who led her to the Episcopal Church. When Rhonda was in the eighth grade, she decided that her religious education at this school meant so much to her that she was confirmed, and Arthurine and Kenny had no choice but to follow her. This has also been the experience of most well loved and successful teachers. You teach a little, but if you stay alert, you will learn even more and are led to into new territories by your own students and children as Arthurine so often was.

"All who are led by the Spirit of God are children of God . . . and nothing else in all creation will be able to separate us from the love of God in Christ Jesus our Lord."

As a teacher and principal, I know Arthurine must have tried to explain death and resurrection to many of her children who experienced a death in their family at their young age. I wish I could have been there to hear what she said. Maybe some of you who did will tell us. This is what I imagine she would say to the older children: The God of my understanding loves every part of us. "There is more to this life than the limitations of the physical body. Our souls and bodies are held in life and are more beautiful than the most elegant green pastures and still waters. It is our belief that God will always care for our bodies and souls and will preserve our essence into another existence, an existence more significant, more profound, more timeless than the one in which we presently live. In the fullness of time, God will never separate us from each other or let us go."[2] God promises we will dwell in God's house forever.

How would Arthurine describe this relationship to God beyond this life to the younger children she so steadily and firmly led down the path of reverence, respect, and responsibility for these 19 years? I think she might have told a story, perhaps this story.[3] A young girl is dying of cancer. Children who are dying often have a much better sense of their death than we adults do. Finally one afternoon just before dinner, she asks her mother, "What is it like to die, Mother? Does it hurt?" Her mother, as was also true for Arthurine, was given a gift by the Spirit to respond with this answer. "Do you remember before you were sick how you used to play outdoors all day? You would come in, eat supper, and then sit down on the couch in the den to watch television and fall fast asleep. The next morning you would be surprised to wake up in your own bed with your pajamas on. What you did not know was that someone who loved you very much gently picked you up and took you upstairs put your nightclothes on you and tucked you in. That may be what it is like to die. You go to sleep in one room of God's house and you wake up in another; and the way that you get from one place to the other is in the strong arms of a God who loves you more than you can imagine.

"All who are led by the Spirit of God are children of God . . . and nothing else in all creation will be able to separate us from the love of God in Christ Jesus our Lord."

Perhaps Arthurine told another story to preschool children. A kindergartener that deeply loves his grandfather goes to his gravesite for his grandfather's burial. His older brothers and sister, his parents, and older cousins all speak extemporaneously with favorite poems or sayings of their grandfather that they remember. The young boy so much wants to honor the man who has shown him unconditional love more than any other person, but he cannot remember a prayer or a poem. His aunt sings Amazing Grace, and then he knows what he will do. The small boy steps forward in front of the crowd and sings his favorite song to his grandfather . . ." Happy Birthday to you, Happy Birthday to you, Happy Birthday, dear grandpa, Happy Birthday to you." How beautifully God speaks through our children and teaches us theology. Yes, our death indeed is a new birth . . . a new birth-day.

The chaplain of the Cathedral School, Beth Maze, tells us that much of the theology children learn is in the songs they sing, and in difficult times, where there are no words to express feelings, she hears her children singing the songs they have learned at school, at church, at the Christmas pageant, at chapel, or in choir. Today the Cathedral School choristers are doing just that for all of us in the anthems they are singing from the Faure requiem the *Pie Jesu* and *In Paridesum* as well as Brother James Air, a musical adaptation of the 23rd Psalm. Today children and grandchildren of children whom Mrs. Harrison taught and led are expressing to us much better than words I can say the message of resurrection for Arthurine and all of us. Their parents learned in ages past from teachers and leaders like Arthurine and now these children pass it on to us . . . and today they remind us that we very often will "meet these saints who teach and care for us in school or in lanes or at sea, in church or in trains or in shops or at tea."[1]

1. Lesbia Scott, " I sing a song of the saints of God, *Thy Hymnal 1982,* no. 293.
2. Kate Moorehead, "Ash Wednesday," *Organic God,* pp. 3–5.
3. Peter Marshall sermon, "Mother, what is it like to die?" Naval Academy, December 7, 1941, in *A Man Called Peter,* Catherine Marshall, pp. 230–232.

Funeral of Charles Wood, a beloved grandfather

John 5:24–27
St. Margaret's • December 8, 2001

We have come here to celebrate and give thanksgiving for the life of Dr. Charles Wood. We are also gathered in this church that Charles so dearly loved as friends and family suffering a great loss. The grief is sometimes unbearable.

How meaningful that Charles would die on December 6, the feast day of St. Nicholas, a man known for his love of his children, his great faith, and his charity and kindness to others. Charles was indeed a Nicholas to his family . . . and to so many others . . . a Nicholas to his many patients he listened to and comforted with his very wise and kind words.

We think today especially of Charles' two grandchildren, Cole Gaston, his namesake, and Emily. How do you tell these precious children that someone who cared so much for them has gone on to eternal life, and it may be some time before they will ever see him again as he once appeared to them. How do you explain that eternal life is different from immortality? Immortality means you never die. That is what we believed when we were *teenagers*. Eternal life is a new life, moving into a new room, different from the past. Eternal life is new life, not more of the same old life.[1] How do we tell these precious children that "dying is not a PERIOD at the end of a sentence, but a COMMA, where we die and go on to a new relationship with God AND with those we love?"

There is so much about this new life that is a mystery. How I wish there were more about it in scripture.[2] Couldn't Jesus have spent a little more time telling us what this eternal life would be like. I wish we could have had some eyewitness stories about life after death . . . from Jarius' daughter, or the widow's son, or Lazarus . . . those three people Jesus brought back from the dead. Maybe just a paragraph from them about what eternal life was like . . . but their words and experiences are not recorded.

We do know a little about the resurrected Jesus. When Jesus was raised from the dead, he did not bring us back any pictures of a place. All he brought back was himself in person. The resurrected Jesus did not resume his previous life. There is nothing in the Gospels that implies that he died and then came back and carried on "as usual." He did not seem confined to time and space. He would appear and disappear. Sometimes his closest followers, like Mary Magdalene could not recognize him until he called her specifically by name.

The disciples who meet Jesus after the resurrection on the road to Emmaus did not recognize him as he walked and unbelievably explained the scriptures to them UNTIL he also ate with them.

And so here we are today so much like those friends on the road to Emmaus . . . grieving the loss of someone we so deeply love, our best friend, the close companion on whom we counted for everything, the one we did learn so much from when we ate with him at those special family meals which were so important to him. Like our brother and sister on the road to Emmaus, we cry out, "are you the only one who does not know that Charles Wood has died. . . ."

Like Mary Magdalene, like those on the road to Emmaus, we will know that both Charles and Christ are here with us, but for some reason we often will not recognize them. We will talk to them in prayer, especially at meals and at Eucharist. Sometimes we will truly feel them both beside us. Sometimes it will be more difficult, but they will be there. Those whom we love are always near, in death as in life.

"We are told that the light we see in the night sky is the light of a star long since dead, but the light reaches us and leads us on. We are not surprised therefore, when a light stranger than the light of any star falls across our way, warming us, leading us, and pointing us to a world beyond anything that we can see. The light is real; we know where it comes from, and we can look for the life of the world to come."

Nancy, Cathy, Suzanne, your experience tells you that God loves you so much that he brought you to live with Charles who especially loved the three of you more than I can describe. Our experience tells us that this God would not just let this love stop with Charles' death. The love of Jesus reached out to you in the life of Charles and will still embrace you in his life beyond death.

Charles in his love taught us all so very much in his life about kindness, wisdom, strength. In his DYING he also taught all of us how to LIVE, to live valiantly, courageously, a warrior to the end.

It is impossible to believe that Charles, his strength, his love and his magnificent intelligence are extinguishable. The God of our understanding would not do this. There is something about a person like Charles that no cancer, no blast of wind can blow out. In this mysterious universe we know that those who mean most to us mean EVEN MORE to God. In God's way, he will keep them, and because he keeps them, we will never be separated from them, or they from us.

So, what do we say to Emily and Cole? Emily, do you remember the year you started to school? Remember that first day of school and how new and exciting everything was? You were the same little girl, but all of a sudden, everything in your life was quite different. Death too is the beginning of something new and different. That's what it is like right now for Charles, like starting to a new school. . and goodness knows you know he will LOVE IT, for he so loved to learn and share his knowledge with others . . . and somehow we know he will still be sharing that new knowledge with the rest of us.

Why did Jesus not tell us more about this resurrected life? Perhaps there ARE not words to describe eternal life. Perhaps it would be like . . . describing to someone who has been blind from birth/ the sunset you saw, Cathy, the night your father died.

But wait a moment, let's do what Charles would have done and think and read scripture a little more carefully to see if there is something there about this new life. Does not Jesus tell us over and over again what eternal life is like /and we just keep missing it? Matthew calls it the kingdom of Heaven "is like" . . . Mark and Luke call it the Kingdom of God "is like" . . . All of these passages are telling us about eternal life.

"Jesus said, "Very truly, I tell you, anyone who hears my word and believes him who sent me has eternal life." In this gospel we read today, John (17) is telling us that eternal life is knowing God, being and staying in relationship with God. DO YOU REALIZE WHAT THIS MEANS? "Eternal life does not start when we are dead. We will have glimpses of it in this life . . . with the promise of even more . . . The promise of eternal life is not merely for when we die. It is for right now." We all learned this from Charles as he shared his relationship with God with so many of us. This is his legacy to us. He shared with us many tastes of this heavenly relationship and we have do doubt that he now even more lives this life eternal he so much believed in.

Charles also taught us about the new life that we call resurrection. Several years ago, after his encounter with heart disease, his life was resurrected, dramatically changed. Resurrection also does not have to be a one-time event at the end of life. It can be a more frequent occurrence. Charles taught us that. We welcome it, but we also dread it, for it is always preceded by a death" of some sort. Life as Charles' lived, in the reality of the resurrection is a miracle, a miracle he shared with us.

"Some say that when the body dies, life goes. Our experience is when the body dies that life goes on. This was Christ's gift to us. We know this is true because he has told us and we also know it because he has shown us in his life and in the lives of so many others that are still going on." Charles deeply believed this.

"Today we give thanks for the life of Charles Wood, who to us was a tower of strength, who stood by us and helped us; who cheered us by his sympathy and encouraged us by his example; who looked not on the outward appearance, but lovingly into the hearts of men and women and children; who rejoiced to serve others; whose loyalty was steadfast, whose friendship was unselfish and secure; whose joy it was to be of service. May Charles find abiding peace in God's heavenly kingdom; and with God's help, may we carry forward his unfinished work for Christ on this earth."[3] Amen

1. Edward Gleason, *Dying We Live,* 76, 84,144.
2. Theodore Farris, *Death and Transfiguration.*
3. J. B. Bernardin, *Funeral Services,* p.117.

Funeral for Forrest Pollard, founding member of St. Luke

February 1, 2013

There is a very holy chapel at Kanuga, an Episcopal retreat and conference center, near Ashville, North Carolina. Like our chapel at Camp Mitchell, this sacred place of worship is called the Chapel of Transfiguration. The chapel was built in 1936 of Carolina white pine from trees taken down in an ice storm that year. The building began shortly after the storm, and the wood was not pretreated. Now over three quarters of a century later as you look at the walls and especially the ceiling you see strange oval and oblong dark marks that are most prominent and numerous at the highest part of the ceiling. Examining closer you realize that these are fingerprints embedded in the wood from the oil in the hands of workers who built the sacred space. The chapel was not insulated so supposedly the mountain winter cold and the summer heat stained these marks even more prominently and permanently. The fingerprints are most prevalent at areas in the chapel where the workmanship was the most difficult, as in the ceiling.

As I talked to Forrest Pollard's family and friends, these were uniformly the first remarks, "the fingerprints of Francis and Forrest Pollard are all over St. Luke's." Since this church is insulated and not made from untreated Carolina white pine, you cannot see these fingerprints, but they are here prominently and permanently and made most numerous during times when their ministry was most needed. And now the earthly bodies of both of these beloved members of St. Luke's are permanently here in our columbarium. Francis, Forrest, Ann, and David were some of the earliest members of St. Luke's. Forrest and Francis believed in instilling in their children that church was one of the most important parts of life. Ann's godparents were Mary Glenn and Rudy Bangert, the second rector of St. Luke's. David was an acolyte in the Fortenberry House. David's Eagle Scout project was the sidewalk by the Fortenberry House where our present offices are. David was the fixer when anything went wrong at the church. Forrest served on the vestry, was junior and senior warden, taught numerous classes. Francis was administrative assistant to Lawson Anderson, the third rector of St. Luke's. Ed Seward and Travis Heard, you will be glad to know that Forrest was the one who almost daily watered the lawn and left it in such good condition for you. Our Library is dedicated to Francis and contains over 1000 books, most of them from Forrest. Forrest was an avid reader especially of philosophy and religious history and prompted others to read as well, especially his children. He would immerse himself in a subject and learn everything possible about it. He studied Judaism to such an extent that Ann and David were certain that he had decided to convert. But then Forrest studied the Moslem religion just as intensely. Forrest taught EfM with the same passion.

Forrest was also known for being "the devil's advocate." He wanted to make certain that he and those around him looked at all the sides of an issue. This was a gift to his children, teaching them to question, explore, search before making a decision. Of course this often added extra hours to vestry meetings and made annual meetings more interesting. Ann has been told by several people, "Your dad is now up in heaven, arguing with God." Her response is, "No, he already did that on earth."

Forrest had a dry sarcastic sense of humor. Ann recalls a time one week when she forgot to write her parents when she was away at college. Her father calls and asks, "Ann, your mother wants to know how your broken arm is doing." Forrest loved his family and was dedicated to Francis, taking her to every appointment for the painful two years before her death. Forrest was immensely proud of his children and instilled in them a love of knowledge and education, agreeing to pay for whatever education they wanted. Forrest's sister, Jeanette, also talks about how he helped pay for her education as well. He had an incredible work ethic taking on each study and job with a passion, receiving a PhD in Business Administration, and rising to be a professor of Economics and Marketing at UALR. Ann remembers also that her father instilled in her brother and herself a legacy of not seeing any difference in gender or color of people in general but particularly people you work with.

Forrest was known about St. Luke's for telling wonderful stories, war stories, stories from history, stories about St. Luke's. He could tell you anything you wanted to know about every county in Arkansas, its history and prominent families. He was a walking encyclopedia of Arkansas demographics. It was a given that when Forrest began to talk, like the former brokerage firm EF Hutton, "people listened." I know Ann and David and Travis and Colin would love to hear more of your stories about Forrest at the reception after this service.

After Forrest retired his new office became the Waffle House where he and our beloved Denny Langlais met and decided how to make the world a better place before they went to work on St. Luke's Library.

I got to know Forrest as his sight and his hearing were declining. I often don't think he heard me, but when we did Eucharist together, he continually said, "Thank you, thank you, thank you." I am certain that he knew that the meaning of the Greek root word for eucharist, εὐχαριστία, means "thank you, thank you, thank you." Ann believes that Forrest missed hearing music the most in his deafness, but losing his sight was the most difficult when he could no longer read. This is so hard ever to understand when people we love lose the very gifts that have brought so much meaning to their lives and to others.

Ann and David, how do we work through the death of someone who was such an important figure in your life? My experience is that the God of our understanding never gives us a loving and important relationship and then suddenly takes it away. Death is not a period at the end of a sentence, but more like a comma.

You can kiss your family good-bye as each of you did at UAMS on Tuesday, but at the same time you carry Francis and now Forrest with you in your heart, your mind, your stomach, because you do not just live in a world, but a world lives in you.

The Presbyterian minister, Frederick Buechner, has written much about the death of a father, a brother, his own in particular. His experience is that these giants[1] of our childhood like your father, Ann and David, like your grandfather, Colin and Trevor, like your brother, Jeanette, live on.

They seem so well to manage to take even death in stride because although death can put an end to their earthly life as we know it, it can never put an end to your relationship with them. They are alive in the resurrection, but without doubt they also are still alive in you.

Memory is more than a looking back to a time that is no longer; it is a looking out into an altogether different kind of time, a new heaven and a new earth, a house where there are many dwelling places; it is looking out into another kind of time where everything that ever was continues not just to be, but to grow and change with the life of those who have died, who in some mysterious way are alive in the resurrection and also still alive in us. The people we loved; the people who loved us; the people who, for good or ill, taught us things; especially in their death, will we begin to understand them in new ways. In some

38

mysterious way they also come to understand us—and through them we also come to understand ourselves and them—in new ways.

Who knows what "the communion of saints" means, but surely it means more than just that we are all haunted by ghosts, because they are not ghosts, but a cloud of witnesses. Those in the resurrection we once knew are not just echoes of voices that have for years ceased to speak. They are saints in the sense that through them something of the power and richness of their life that touched us in the past, now continues to touch us in new ways.

They have their own business to get on with now, I assume— "increasing in knowledge and love of You," says the Book of Common Prayer, and moving "from strength to strength in the life of perfect service in your kingdom," which all sounds like business enough for anybody. We can imagine all of us on this shore fading from them as they journey ahead toward whatever new shore may await them; but it is as if they carry something of us on their way as we assuredly carry something of them on our journey. This perhaps is why we are gradually called not only to remember them as they used to be but to see and hear them in some new sense. If they had things to say to you then, they also have things to say to you now, and what they say may not always be what you will expect or the same things you have heard from them before.[1]

Be open to this experience.
Buechner says this is some of what he thinks they are saying to you.

When you remember us, it means you are carrying something of us with you and that we have left some marks, our fingerprints on you, just as we have left our fingerprints on St. Luke's. Marks, fingerprints of who you are and who we are. You will summon us back to your mind countless times. This means that even after we die, you can still see our faces and hear our voices and speak to us in your mind and in your heart . . . and someday, as in the resurrection of our Lord, you will see us again, face to face."[2]

1. Frederick Buechner, "How They Do Live On," originally in *The Sacred Journey,* January 1, 2013, *Buechner Quote of the Day.*
2. Frederick Buechner, *Whistling in the Dark,* 110–111.

Funeral of Marie Garnett, my aunt, interpreting a relative, a free spirit

We come to honor the life of Marie Garnett, the youngest child of James and Elizabeth Johnson. Marie and Hugh were the lone survivors of their generation. Marie's brother, Bud, and his wife Florence and Marie's older sister, Mildred, and her husband, Joel preceded her in death. In fact, shortly Marie's body will be buried near her parents and her sister, Mildred, and her husband. Now it is our generation, Liz and Charlie, Jim and Cece, Steve and Janie who have become the older generation. It is time, for this brief moment, for us, our children and our grandchildren to stop and ponder the legacy of this family and what parts we want to carry forward, what parts we want to leave behind? How do we honor our heritage? What have we learned from the lives of those who gave us life and now are in a different relationship with us and God?

A predominant heritage of our family is a deep and abiding faith. Six members of this family are in some form of ministry, three ordained, and I suspect there will be more before it is all over. Ministry

Others have experimented with nontraditional faiths and they have been accepted. Acceptance: another strength of this family. Acceptance to become the person God has called you to be. I don't think anyone has ever been thrown out of the family . . . yet.

A strong commitment to education and service. Certainly Elizabeth and James Johnson must have played that education record every night as Bud, Marie, and Mildred went to bed and I think it was still playing in the morning when they awoke . . . and they made a tape that Bud, and Marie, and Mildred played for us and now we hand it over as a CD to our children and grandchildren. This family has at least seven educators and teachers and five in the healing professions. We also have two fitness experts, 2 pilots, a musician, a banker, a world-class soccer coach, a scientist, a computer expert, a lumberman, one lawyer, two archivists, three counselors, a chef, an environmentalist, and two foresters. What a legacy.

I ran out of fingers and toes trying to count all the degrees in this family. Needless to say, I must use a medical term to describe them . . . TNC . . . too numerous to count.

Three members of our family, Elizabeth, Mildred, and Marie died with some form of dementia . . . beautiful, brilliant, loving, productive minds, destroyed, gone blank by some unknown silent enemy. It remains the fear of all the rest of us here, that this could be our end as well and this is not what we would choose. These three women have taught all of us that we do not choose our end and much of the time it makes no sense. But then again, how much of life is reasonable, how little control we have over our life. Our lives are not in our hands, but God's, and we are living an illusion if we think we are in control. These three women in our family have taught us how very precious each moment of our life is, and how we should treasure it. The precious present . . . a gift from God to be opened daily and lived and enjoyed and shared.

Free Spirit. Each generation of this family also has had a free spirit. Marie was certainly the free spirit of her generation. What we have learned from free spirits is that when they soar, their flight is beautiful and they teach us things about life that the rest of us "down to earthlings" never dreamed existed. We have also learned that their fall from flight can be very painful for both them and us. Our free spirits keep us on our toes, keeping us from the dull humdrum life. They can bring unbelievable joy to life, but also they sometimes bring deep sorrow. Our family has decided to take "the road less traveled," and let the free spirits live among us and teach us things we otherwise would never know about them, ourselves, and God our Creator, who has made each one of us so very different.

Each one of us has a little piece of God within us. Our job is to connect to God within us. Sometimes this takes a lifetime. But when we do make this connection to a higher power, the Creator within, the Holy Spirit, the Christ, it is sooo unbelievable. We want to go and tell the world, our friends, our family that we have found God. However, we must remember we only have knowledge, intimacy, awareness of a little piece of God. The next part of our journey, and this certainly is a lifetime exploration, is to connect our knowledge of God, our piece of God with our neighbor, each person we meet each day. We must look for and connect and honor the presence of God in each other. When this happens, our God does not stay small but becomes huge. It is like fitting parts of a puzzle together, adding and putting our puzzle part with others to see a much larger image of God. The free spirits of our family often have their piece of God way out on the edge where they often live. We usually don't see their part for some time, not until we have found many other connections, the image of God in so many others, when we journey toward the edge, and we realize that this also is God . . . this also is

God . . . and we see a beautiful part of God that we might have missed if we had not remained on this journey together and stayed connected.

This all became so much clearer to me two days ago when our youngest grandchild, Gray, was baptized. I did not bring my liturgical vestments with me, but instead brought his baptismal gown. It was hand made by our grandmother and I was baptized in it by our grandfather in Clifton Forge I believe. I am sure that my parent's and Liz's and Liz and Marie and Hugh were there as well that Sunday. Some of you may have also been baptized later in this gown as well. Our children and all of our grandchildren have also worn it and I know many more will as well on that special day when we each are acknowledged as a child of God living into the family of God. Gray's baptism was not at a Methodist church or even an Episcopal church. The word of God preached by the priest who baptized Gray is often different from the God of my understanding. But last Sunday morning as I sat in this Lutheran school supporting a newly formed church, through the images of our family and the heritage in this gown, I could not feel our differences but only our connections. I knew we were all connected to a very loving God who cares so deeply for us. That connection cannot be broken. The support and love of this family has been instrumental in constantly reminding me of that relationship.

May God continue to hold this family in the palm of his hand. May we all know and feel God's presence with us moment by moment, and may be feel and know the presence of Marie and all those in our family who are no longer with us in their physical appearance but remain close by our side spiritually. Have you not felt this presence with you? Have you not been given the strength and courage to do something you never thought you would be able to accomplish? When I have experienced this, I have often felt our Grandmother Johnson close beside me, praying me through it (and sometimes even sending that little extra cash that suddenly materialized in a letter from her. We are all still looking for her printing press, which she used to make the money she sent each of us).

Our family is still there close to us; we are constantly surrounded by "a great cloud of witnesses." They are all there lifting us up and supporting us and praying for us . . . and goodness knows we all still need their prayers to carry out the legacy they have set before us.

Funeral for Carolyn Clayton. She died from Cancer but also had a near death experience

John 14:1–6
Christ Church • February 5, 2013

"When[1] Jesus sits down to eat for the last time with his closest friends, he knows it is the last time. You don't have to be the Messiah to know it—they all know it. The Romans are out to get him. The Jews are out to get him. He knows that his time is almost over, and they soon will not be together again.

It is an unforgettable scene in that upper room, the shadows, the stillness, the hushed voices of people speaking very carefully, very intently because they want to get it all said while there is still time and to get it said right.

That night must have haunted the disciples for the rest of their lives as they retell it in so many accounts, including today's passage from John. But the Last Supper is haunting in another way, a kind of shadowy dream, a foreshadowing of an event for all of us, our own last supper, the last time we will sit down with our family, our closest friends. Many people don't know how precious that supper is, how precious these friends are we sit down with for the last time."[1] But Carolyn Clayton knew. Carolyn had a great deal of insight into last suppers. She battled against an aggressive leiomyosarcoma for months. She knew how precious her time was with her many friends and family, her younger sister Donna, her children Tim, Cristen, Clayton, six grandchildren and one great-grandchild.

Today our community sings out with Carolyn Clayton stories. Carolyn touched and connected with so many lives in our state with her courage, her love, her unselfishness, her love and service to our community, and her love for wonderful food and music. I first learned of Carolyn's love of food when I saw her on television recommending Takizi's Mediterranean Restaurant. Carolyn also touched so many lives in her work at Stepping Stone for at-risk youth, as a coordinator for SCAN, as executive director of the Pulaski County American Cancer Society, as Director of Communications and Public Relations at St. Vincent's, but of course her special love was her last job as Executive Director of the Pulaski County Medical Society for the last 13 years.

Carolyn lived much of her life on the Prairie, the Arkansas Prairie, in Prairie

County in a musical family, her father was a tenor, her mother a soprano, and baby sister Donna was an alto. Carolyn soon learned she also had a special gift, her voice. She was a coloratura soprano. That means she had a range from middle C to high F. On the Prairie Carolyn grew up as an Episcopalian singing at St. Peter-on-the Prairie, Tollville, later at St. Stephens Episcopal Church, Jacksonville, St. Luke's North Little Rock, Trinity Cathedral, St. Mark's Episcopal Church as well as two churches on Okinawa when she lived in Japan. Carolyn also was the first lay minister to serve the chalice at St. Peter's.

Carolyn was well known for her realism and wit, which always came with a loving laughing huge smile. Several months ago she had an air conditioner put in. The service man wanted to know did she want a ten-year or a five-year warranty. "Heavens no," dramatically laughs Carolyn as she lifts back her head. "I'm dying of cancer and I don't want to talk about extended warranty."

In[1] the shadowy upper room, the disciples eat their last meal together. They drink the wine Jesus says is his blood and eat the bread he says is his body. Then our friend Thomas courageously asks the question they all have never dared ask before. "Lord, we do not know where you are going. How can we know the way?" As if they do not know. He is going where all of us are going. He is going down the stairs, out the door, into the night. He is going to pray in a garden to the God he calls Father not to let this awful thing happen to him.[1] I know Carolyn prayed near many gardens. Carolyn prayed that this cup would pass, but she also had an experience that told her where Jesus was going and where she was going if this battle with her unusual cancer did not go the way we all hoped. When Carolyn's daughter, Kristin, was born, Carolyn almost died and had a near death experience not unlike that of recent author, Dr. Eben Alexander in his book, *Proof of Heaven, a Neurosurgeon's Journey into the Afterlife.* Carolyn's experience was that she was above all the people in the room in some place that was jeweled and like Julian of Norwich, she continually said, "all shall be well, all shall be well." Carolyn remembers that the message was not only to let her family know that she was well, but that they were well also. How similar is this to Alexander's near-death experience while he was in a coma for a week. Dr. Alexander says he saw millions of butterflies instead of jewels as he traveled with a woman who gave him three messages: "You are loved and cherished, dearly, forever, You have nothing to fear", and There is nothing you can do wrong."[2]

After this experience Carolyn knew the answer to Thomas' question, "Lord, where are you going?", the question within a question. "Lord, are you going anywhere at all or just going out, like a light with no longer any connection to us."

"In John's passage Jesus' answer to us is: "Do not let your hearts be troubled. I go to prepare a place for you. I will come again and will take you with me so that where I am you may be also." We are going to stay connected! " Like so few of us, Carolyn knew and lived this answer in her life. She kept reminding me of her favorite quotation on her Facebook page, "The purpose of the story is to change the beginning by the end." And she had had a taste of the end.

"We are believers,[1] you and I, that's why we are here. At least we are would be believers, part-time believers, believers sometimes with our fingers crossed. Believing IN him is not the same as believing things ABOUT him such as was he born of a virgin or did he raise Lazarus from the dead. Believing IN him is a matter of giving our hearts to him, connecting to Him, turning our life and our will over to him, the way a child believes in a mother or a father; the way a mother or a father believes in a child.

Frederick Buechner talks about the time his only brother died.[1] He finds himself one summer afternoon missing his connection to his brother, needing him so much that he decides to phone his brother's empty New York apartment. He knows perfectly well there is no one there to answer, and yet who could say at least some echo of him might still be there, and he would hear him again, hear the sound, the music in his voice, his marvelous laugh. So there out by his garden in the sunshine, someone who should know better lets the phone ring, lets it ring, lets it ring. Does his brother answer? How wonderful to be able to say that by some miracle he does; but he does not. All he hears is the silence of his absence. Yet who knows? Who can ever know about this great mystery.

Jesus says, "In my Father's house are many dwelling places, many rooms." Both Buechner[1] and I know Carolyn would believe that in one of those many rooms that phone rings and rings true, connects, and is heard. His brother's voice is in the search, in the ringing itself, the attempt for connection, just as Jesus' voice, Jesus' presence also is in the searching, the seeking, the ringing, our attempts at connection.

Jesus says, "I go to prepare a place for you . . . so that where I am you may be also." He says he is not just going out like a light.[1] He says he is going on, going ahead. He says WE will go there as well and stay connected to him and to each other and be dearly loved. Who can resist giving your heart to him who loves you so much that he makes this promise of connection in a place with room enough for everyone whom love unites?

Thomas answers, "Lord, we do not know where you are going; how can we know the way?" Thomas speaks for all of us in our sadness and frustration when we think death has disconnected us from a dear friend like Carolyn.

"I am the way, and the truth, and the life" is Jesus' answer. He[1] doesn't say the church or religion is the way, not even the religion that bears his name. He says he himself is the way, the life, the truth, the connection to each other and God. And the life and truth we are dazzled by, haunted by, nourished by in him is this life that is so full of interconnection, aliveness, music, truth, light, love that not even the darkness of death can disconnect us.

"How do we go where he is?[1] How do we who sometimes just have a hard time finding our way home in the night find the way, the life, the connection that is his way?"

I think Carolyn's life would say we keep on ringing and ringing and ringing,[1] as she did throughout her whole life, because that ringing, the longing, the searching, the seeking, the reaching out of ourselves, the intuition that keeps us at it, that is the connection drawing us to our God transcendent, and our God eminent in each of us. We are to try to draw near to God and to each other, in all possible connections and reconnections, in community, in meals, in service to others as Carolyn learned on the Prairie, by loving, listening for, believing like Carolyn against all odds in the haunting music in this mystery, that the truth of the life of Jesus Christ is that we are all his disciples, we are all his brothers and sisters, and He calls us to connect our lives each precious moment, today and throughout all eternity.[1]

And we shall stay connected even to those we love who have died. And all shall be well, and all shall be well.

---

1. Frederick Buechner, "Let Jesus Show," *Secrets in the Dark*, pp. 265–271.
2. Eben Alexander, *Proof of Heaven, a Neurosurgeon's Journey into the Afterlife*, p. 71.

Funeral for Roger Hinderer
Gentleman and a Seeker

John 14:1–6
Trinity Cathedral • October 30, 2010

"Lord, we do not know where you are going. How can we know the way?" Several years ago I received a call from Mr. Hinderer inviting me to come over for a visit. After the small talk and on the second cup of tea, I realize he wanted to discuss in essence this same question that Thomas asked the night before Jesus died. "Where, Lord are you going. How can we know the way?" It is obvious when you walk into the Hinderer's home, that Mr. Hinderer is a seeker, a life long student, a deep thinker, and an avid reader. The walls of his home are covered with books, especially history books. Classical music plays softly in the background. His apartment is on an upper floor at the level of treetops, like living high in a tree house, the perfect place to drink tea and meditate and think and talk about what this life and the resurrected life are all about. Mr. Hinderer had already made some decisions. He was giving his body to science, but he wanted to know more about what was coming next. We read through the prayer book and even looked at verses in the Bible. My best answer, however, was, "if anyone is certain what the resurrected life is like, be suspect. There is only one who is from there who has come back to tell us about it."

Only once does Jesus directly describe heaven. Sadducees challenge Jesus as they question which man a woman who had seven husbands would be with in the resurrection. Jesus says that in the resurrection all are alive, but in some different state of relationship. They are like angels and are God's children. Things that are of the utmost importance on earth are no longer of such importance.

Resurrection is also different from immortality where life just keeps going on. The resurrected Jesus was the same but different. He was present in his physical body but he would move in and out of locked doors, and close acquaintances did not recognize him until he allowed them to know him.

The Bible does not answer most of our questions about resurrection. It refuses to approach resurrection as something rational. Jesus mentions these many dwelling places in his Father's house and Revelation describes a psychedelic throne room and a cubed jewel box of a city in which every tear is washed away. The Bible talks about resurrection as a mystical thing, based not on our belief in God but on God's belief in us. Any one who is ever part of God's life never stops being part of it.

In this mysterious universe we know that those who mean most to us mean EVEN MORE to God. In God's way, God will keep them, and because God keeps them, we will never be separated from them, or they from us.

I wasn't certain if Mr. Hinderer was satisfied with our conversation, for perhaps a year later, he invited Jason Alexander over to discuss the same questions. I was not offended, however, for this was just one more sign that we were on a journey with a real seeker for answers to questions that so few ever consider. It was a privilege to be seeking with him.

As it became more difficult for Mr. Hinderer to come to church we had more conversations over the phone, but my heart always leaped for joy when I saw him at church. His presence brought something mystical to the service, perhaps because I was aware of his seeking and also I had some inkling of how difficult it was for him to come.

Mr. Hinderer would have been 94 years old this month, but we never guessed his age until we saw it in his obituary. He was still seeking, still trying to read until his death even though his eyesight was failing, a great loss to such an avid reader.

As is so often the case, I learned even more about this remarkable man and his wife shortly after he died.

Mrs. Hinderer told me how they met 64 years ago. The both worked at Herpelshimer's Department Store in Grand Rapids, Michigan in 1946. She smiled at him one day. He went back to the store that night and looked up her personnel file, got her phone number and called her, but she was not home. Roger then came into Louise's office the next day and asked her out. They had one date and they both knew this was it. They were engaged three weeks later and married three months later. Louise, you and Roger defied all the rules of how to have a long lasting and happy marriage and proved all the experts, including the church, wrong! Louise tells me that in their 64 years of marriage, Roger never forgot a birthday or an anniversary and always picked the present out himself. Louise tells me, "We were married for 64 years, but it was not long enough. People tell me they are sorry that Roger has died. I tell them, yes sorry for me, for I will miss him, but not sorry for him. He has made it. "

Jesus says, " Do not let your hearts be troubled. Believe in God, believe also in me. In my Father's house are many dwelling places. If it were not so, would I have told you that I go to prepare a place for you? And if I go and prepare a place for you, I will come again and will take you to myself so that where I am there you may be also."

My words to you, Louise are, my belief is that resurrection is God's way of creating a new heaven and a new earth without doing away with the old heaven and the old earth. It is God's way to redeem and reclaim this world, to take what we have messed up and make it right again. The resurrection is God's unwillingness to let us go, because God loves his creation that much. Perhaps we will later find our beloved in the resurrection and understand at once they never left us.

Louise, this belief is reinforced by your last night together. We have some insight into the answers to Mr. Hinderer's questions about resurrection in his last words to you. As Louise leaves his room, Roger whispers to her, " I love you. I will be waiting for you."

Funeral Virginia Schall
Died in her 95th Year

St. Luke's Episcopal • Church June 10, 2013

In just six more months, on December 20th of this year Virginia would have been 95 years old. I invite you to go back in your imagination to that date December 20, 1918, the day Virginia was born. The First World War had just ended on November 11, a little over a month ago. When Virginia was a little over one year old, January 1920, the 18th amendment went into effect banning the sale of alcohol in this country. It was not until December 1933, when Virginia was almost 13 when the 21st amendment was passed allowing the sale of alcohol. Virginia was not quite two years old when the 19th amendment was ratified and women were allowed to vote on August 1920. Virginia was not quite 11 when the stock market crashed on October 29, 1929. She was barely 23 years old when World War II started on December 7, 1941. She was 35 when this church, St. Luke's was founded on March 31, 1954.

Thank you Gary for telling us about what happened during and after some of these times in Virginia's life. Jean Belknap reminded me that it was not until Virginia's 90th birthday party that Jean's husband and Virginia's doctor, Melvin, talked Virginia into stop driving her car. I wish I could have heard Virginia play the violin or known some of the dogs she and Billy so loved especially "Chitty Chitty Bang Bang" whose death I have heard was announced in the prayers of the people here at St. Luke's. My experience with Virginia was that she was an amazing fighter about leaving this life. I have never seen anyone so determined not to die. I wonder if she learned her survival skills by living through all the tumult of her times, some of which we have honored by remembering. I hope some of you have heard more of her stories of these times that she has lived in and can remember these stories and tell it to the rest of us and to your children and grandchildren.

Remember. Remember. This is at the core of our faith. "Remember that you are dust and to dust you shall return," we hear on Ash Wednesday.

The anthems Carey read at the beginning of this service, and what he will read at the end are a remembrance. Our scripture readings we have just heard are a remembrance; the apostle's creed we will soon say is a remembrance. Our

Eucharist is a remembrance. Soon Carey will say, "thine only Son Jesus Christ did institute, and in his holy gospel command us to continue a perpetual memory of that his precious death and sacrifice, until his coming again." "Take, eat, this is my Body, which is given for you. Do this in remembrance of me." "Do this, as oft as ye shall drink it, in remembrance of me." "We, . . . now offer before thee, the memorial thy Son hath commanded us to make; having in remembrance his blessed passion and precious death, his mighty resurrection. ."

Remember. Listen closely to this word, re-member, to bring back to the group, bring back to the whole, to become a member again.

Memory brings those who have died back to life.[1] Remembering is a living metaphor for eternal life. Metaphor is one of the best ways we have left to approach God, and remembering is that living metaphor for eternal life. Loss brings pain, but pain triggers memory, and memory is a kind of new birth within each of us. It is that new birth after long pain that becomes resurrection, remembering, that to our surprise comforts us. We will have pain, but God gives us memory to change pain to laughter, to joy, to bring the dead back into our lives, to comfort us, to make us understand that living metaphor. The brief vividness of our memories of loved ones who have died is a sign of the life God restores in resurrection. Even in dementia we lose recent memory, but the past stays with us and can comfort us.

Frederick Buechner writes[2] that, "When you REMEMBER me, it means that you have carried something of who I am with you, that I have left some mark of who I am on who you are. It means that you can summon me back to your mind even though countless years and miles may stand between us. It means that when we meet again, you will know me. It means that even after I die, you can still see my face and hear my voice and speak to me in your heart."

Our faith is founded on remembering.

Today we remember and celebrate the life of Virginia in the house where she came to remember Jesus and his promise to her of resurrection and eternal life.

1. Sue Miller, "While I Was Gone," *Listening for God, vol. 4,* p. 66.
2. Frederick Buechner, *Whistling In the Dark,* p. 110–111.

Funeral for Sylvia Hagood,
Saying Goodbye to a Lay Minister

John 11:21–27
St. Margaret's • May 16, 2007

As we said our goodbyes to Sylvia in ICU, Peggy reminded us of all those bedsides that Sylvia had sat by and said goodbyes and prayers for the dying, often when family members could not be present. I know many of you have been there when Sylvia visited the sick and dying as well. Actually I am a little irritated at Sylvia, because I was planning on her being with me when I die, for I knew she would know better than anyone else what to do and say. Friday afternoon I kept expecting her to wake up and sit up in bed in ICU and remind us of something we had forgotten to do or tell one of the hospital personnel to leave us alone, that we were busy.

Sylvia was an icon, a role model of someone who took her spirituality with her wherever she went, but especially to her work. Sylvia was a nurse par excellence. I loved going to the hospital with her, for she would go into a room to make a pastoral care visit and then out to the nursing station and tell them, this was needed, this wasn't right. She was pastor, nurse, and social worker all rolled up into a compact bundle of energy. There was no separation of her roles. They were all intertwined. She was a delicious combination of Mary and Martha.

We loved her honesty and forthrightness. Her last words to me as I walked out of her room were, "I like your new hair color." We knew what to expect when we were with her. No hidden agendas. Her life had been too much of a struggle for hidden agendas. Hidden agendas are too time consuming.

Sylvia deeply loved her family Doug, Robert, Ellen, Susan and her two grandchildren Darcy and Jack. You were the great joy of her life. As Robert was saying goodbye to his mother, he told me he said to her, "Job well done, good and faithful servant." Our priest tells us that, perhaps our friends tell us that, but when your children say that to you, I think even God is moved to tears.

Sylvia's caring for others, her pastoral care especially at St. Margaret's was phenomenal. I doubt it there is anyone in this room who has not received care and love from her. I began to list the kindnesses she had done for my family, and I had to stop I was so overwhelmed.

You may have known Sylvia as a recipient of her pastoral care. I also knew her also as a scholar. We took so many courses together, Community of Hope, Mourner's Path, Servant Leadership School. She attended all of Chris Keller's, Pat Murray's Peggy's, Dennis', Susan's, and Cindy's classes. Every time there was a course here at St. Margaret's, Sylvia was there. She was on the front row of Peggy's classes about the three interconnected parts of the Christian life: worship, action, and doctrine. Sylvia knew the three-legged stool of Anglican Doctrine: scripture, tradition, and reason. We try to remember this morning what our Anglican teachings said to her and to us about her death.

What does Scripture tell us about Sylvia's death? A few verses later in this gospel from John, we read that Jesus wept at the death of Martha's brother, Lazarus. Jesus is telling us that weeping is what we should do, and all of us today have done much weeping. Today's readings from Isaiah and Revelation also tell us that our God will guide and hold us and personally wipe away these tears.

At his own death Jesus asks his Father, "God where are you?" Jesus is telling us that doubting, arguing, feeling abandoned are feelings just as Christian as feeling held in God's arms. We know today's reading from John is true that "he is the resurrection and the life and that everyone who lives and believes will never die." We know in our minds that Sylvia is experiencing resurrection. But there is a part of our hearts that still wants her here with us physically to tell us in her not so subtle way what we need to be doing.

What does our Tradition tell us about her death?[1] There are many sermons in our tradition by ministers who have experienced the death of a loved one. Karl Barth, Friedrich Schleiermacher William Sloane Coffin Jr, and John Claypool all preached about the death of close family members. It is interesting how all of these towers of faith were shaken to their roots. As they looked for hope, they wrote profusely and vividly about what did not help them in their grieving. One universal dead end theology for these preachers was the often-quoted phrase that the death of someone like Sylvia was God's will. This is not the God of my understanding, and it was not theirs or Sylvia's. After the death of his son in a car accident when the car went off a bridge into the water, William Sloane Coffin preaches, "my own consolation lies in knowing that it was not the will of God that my son die; as the waves closed over his sinking car, God's heart was the first of all our hearts to break." And I think we have all felt God's heart breaking with Sylvia's illness.

All of the preachers finally do find comfort in scripture, but the scripture is different for each of them and not the usual one-liners that we all try to say to comfort one another.[1] Sylvia found comfort in Scripture, and I know our reassurance is there as well. I think Sylvia would tell us to read and look for it, but the words, the verses will be different for each of us. For Sylvia's family the 23rd Psalm has been comforting. Bless her for teaching you that.

And finally what does reason tell us about her death, which really means what is our own experience of grief and death. In our Mourner's Path grief recovery groups, Sylvia often talked about loved ones who had died who were not only in a new relationship to God but also to us. Death changes but does not destroy our communion with the saints, those we love. Sylvia, like Jesus is resurrected and will be with us always throughout all eternity. Her presence no longer depends on time and space.

Sylvia often shared experiences of knowing the presence of loved ones after they died, doing things she knew she had never been able to do before because of some presence very near to her, guiding, still caring for her.

The Old Testament gives us a wonderful description of this experience. As Elijah nears death, he asks his beloved companion, Elisha, "Tell me what I may do for you, before I am taken from you." Elisha responds, " Please let me inherit a double share of your spirit." Elijah says, "You have asked a hard thing."

You know the story. As Elijah ascends in a whirlwind into heaven, he leaves for Elisha his mantle or shawl. That will also be our experience. Sylvia has left us a mantle to wear, a ministry, a way of loving and caring she has modeled so well for us to continue her work.

When our pain is so deep and real that we can not see or feel anything else,/ our scripture, tradition, and reason tell us that though our pain is true, it is not the ultimate truth. We have all seen in Sylvia's life glimpses of the ultimate truth.

This afternoon and for some time to come, we will be telling more Sylvia stories, seeing through the prism of her life and faith both in glad and sorrowful memories, refractions of the grace and love of God. This afternoon we will celebrate her life with her favorite meal, the Eucharist. Our service will then continue to the columbarium where we will sacramentally carry her back to God. In our liturgy we are in effect shouting a prayerful petition to God,[2] "God, get ready! Here comes Sylvia! A sinner of your own redeeming, a lamb of your own flock. You have given her to us and now with gratitude for her life, we are returning her to you. Thank you, God for the privilege of experiencing your love through her. Alleluia. Alleluia, Alleluia!"

1. Jeffrey J. Newlin, "Standing at the Grave," *This Incomplete One,* pp. 121–130.
2. Thomas Long, "O Sing to Me of Heaven: Preaching at Funerals," *Journal for Preachers,* 21–26, vol. 29, no. 3, Easter 2006.

Funeral for Jim Waldron, a tower of strength in recovery

Christ Church • February 13, 2014

"The airport is crowded, noisy, frenetic.[1] There are inconsolable crying babies, people being paged, the usual ruckus. Outside, a mixture of snow and sleet is coming down. The runways show signs of icing. Flight delays and cancellations are called out over the PA system together with the repeated warning that any luggage left unattended will be immediately impounded. There are more people than usual going to designated areas to smoke. Once aboard, you peer through the windows for traces of ice on the wings/ and search the pancaked faces of the flight attendants for any sign of the knot of anxiety you feel in your own stomach while they run by rote through the emergency procedures. The great craft lumbers its way to the take-off position, the jets shrill. As it picks up speed, you count the seconds till you feel liftoff. More than so many seconds, you've heard, means trouble. Once airborne, you can hardly see the wings at all through the gray turbulence scudding by. The steep climb is as rough as a Ford pickup ascending Petit Jean Mountain. Gradually the plane starts to even out. The clouds thin a little. Here and there you see tatters of clear air among them. The pilot levels off slightly. Nobody is talking. The calm, the quiet are almost palpable. Suddenly, in a rush of light, you break out of the weather. Beneath you the clouds are a furrowed pasture. Above, no sky in creation was ever bluer."

Frederick Buechner writes that the very last takeoff as Jim, our dear friend, took on Saturday might be something like that. For weeks Jim was constantly surrounded by family and friends and especially by Liz mid-wifing him through his journey. "We do not know, but when the time finally comes, maybe Jim is scared stiff, but maybe by then he is just as glad to leave the whole show behind and get going on a new adventure, traveling to a new and very different place. Oh, how Jim loves to travel!

Maybe Jim's flight that Saturday morning was something like this: "in a matter of moments, everything that seems to matter may stop mattering. The slow climb is all there is. The stillness. The clouds. Then the miracle of the flight is that you surface suddenly out of dense clouds into open blue sky . . . and there it is . . . The dazzling sun (Son)."

We remember today a man who has just taken this fight and who for many of us was a giant in our lives. Jim has most beautifully been described by his grandson Zach as "a father, son, husband, grandfather, medical doctor, sponsor, yoga instructor, tai chi apprentice, avid reader, world traveler, loved by many—and the legacy he left motivates *us* to continue making a positive impact on the world." For weeks you have been visiting Jim in hospice, having AA and Alanon meetings in his room and sharing Jim stories. I hope you will continue to share today the many ways this man helped you in your recovery or practice. This is my personal Jim story. Jim and I both came into AA about the same time when Cosmo, our home group, was at old St. John's Seminary on Tyler. I remember my first meeting with this quiet man of a few softly spoken words sitting on the back row. There is something very special about the person who comes into recovery near the time you do, especially if he is of the same profession, someone who knows a little of what you are feeling, especially your fears. Jim's first sponsor, Don Browning, was a taskmaster. Mine was not, so I would hear from Jim what I was supposed to be doing and wonder if I ever was going to make it. Jim was a veracious reader, reading especially recovery material every night before going to bed, and asking me what I thought about it, or giving me a new book at our next meeting. Early on Jim and I learned the best way to recover would be to work with others. We hoped to help support other physicians in need of recovery. We both started the first physician health committees at our respective hospitals. Jim became a tower of strength to so many, myself included. Any question about recovery or what to do about a person in recovery I would go to him. I also learned that any question I had about medicine he also knew. Many of you here know that. Jim was a brilliant physician. Did I also mention that he was an amazing cook? Italian food was his specialty. Jim also was an expert guide for new restaurants in our area?

Did I mention how very, very much Jim loved his children and grandchildren?

In recovery Jim and Markie have been leading the Hour of Power on Sunday at Wolfe Street, church for so many in recovery. Also for years Jim and I have been facilitators for the Serenity Retreat, a yearly retreat in early January for those in AA and Alanon at Subiaco Abbey, started twenty-one years ago by Clint Boeshears, and now sponsored by our diocese. Jim continued to be very active at Wolfe Street, the major recovery center in our city and state and most recently has been its president. Jim also brought me along when we met with Larry Benfield over ten years ago to ask permission to use the basement facilities here at Christ Church for AA meetings. Jim stayed very active in this group at noon for those in recovery who work downtown.

I have heard Jim tell his story several times. It is his story, so I cannot repeat him. I can only say he tells of hearing a message/ from somewhere one early morning to make a phone call to seek recovery. He listened to that message, which you and I have no doubt about where it came from, and the rest is history. His life was changed, and the life of each of us here was changed. Jim has been in recovery since April 15 1992, Maundy Thursday of that year. Three days later on Easter Sunday Jim and Liz attended their first meeting together at Hour of Power at Wolfe Street. In years to follow, Jim's sobriety date often also fell on Easter. Jim and Liz answered another phone call around Easter to an open house at St. Margaret's Episcopal Church three years after they both were in recovery. They became active there and joined Christ Church when they moved downtown. I loved Liz's expression when they joined St. Margaret's that she just went 33 years between church services. I hope you are getting my message. These two, Jim and Liz are Christ's Easter people, icons for resurrection in this life and the life to come.

We know so very little about the resurrection life after death, but we have seen in Jim and Liz, what resurrection looks like in this life. They both overcame a death in this life. This helps us believe that the resurrection promised after life indeed also occurs. "The good news of God in Christ is that when the bottom falls out from under us, when we have crashed through all our safety nets and we hear the bottom rushing up to meet us, the good news is that we cannot fall farther than God can catch us. Of course some of us know that we can't always be too picky about how far down the catch occurs. We have seen the miracle in Liz and Jim's lives and have a promise that the miracle happens again with the death of our mortal bodies. The power of the God of our understanding has always been to raise us from the dead now. . in this life and the life to come. Period." It is all about the power of turning our life and will over to God.

In the meantime, how do we stay connected to the ones we love, whom we so miss, who are living in the resurrection? Buechner comforts us in saying:

"those who have died will live on,/ those giants of our life. God will never allow an end to our relationship with them. There is no doubt that Jim lives still in us. The people we loved. The people who loved us. The people who taught us. Even though they may die, my experience is that God continues to lead us to understand them, ourselves, and our relationship in new ways.[2]

Who knows what "the communion of saints" means, but surely it means more than that we are all haunted by ghosts/ because they are not ghosts, these people we once knew and loved are not just echoes of voices that cease to speak, but saints in the sense that through them something of the power and richness of life itself touched us in our lifetime, and God will allow that life to continue to touch us.

We assume Jim has his own business to get on with now—"increasing in knowledge and love of Thee," says the Book of Common Prayer, and moving "from strength to strength," which sounds like business enough for anybody. We can imagine all of us on this shore fading from Jim as he journeys ahead toward whatever new shore awaits him; but it is as if Jim will carry something of us on his way, as we assuredly carry something of him on our journey. God calls us not only to remember those who have died as they used to be, but seeing and hearing them in some new sense that they are becoming. If they said things to us in the past, they may still have things to say to us now, but they may not always be what we will expect.

> "We can kiss our family and friends good-bye and put miles and death between us, but at the same time we carry each other with us in our heart, our mind, our stomach, our soul because we do not just live in a world but a world lives in us."[3]

I think Jim might quote Buechner and say,

> "when you remember me, it means you have carried something of who I am with you, that I have left some mark of who I am on who you are. It means that you can summon me back to your mind even though countless years and miles stand between us. It means that when we Easter people meet again in the resurrection, you will know me. It means that even though I die, you can still see my face and hear my voice and speak to me in your heart." [3]

1. Frederick Buechner, "Dying," Originally published in *Whistling in the Dark,* 41–42 and later in *Beyond Words,* 87–88.

2. Frederick Buechner, "How They do Live On" originally in *The Sacred,* frederickbuechner.com.

3. Frederick Buechner, "Remember," *Whistling in the Dark,* p. 110–11.

Funeral of My brother who died on Boxing Day, the second day of Christmas 2014

Good Shepherd

John 10:11–16
Christ Episcopal Church, Martinsville, Virginia

My brother, your husband, father, uncle, cousin, friend died on Boxing Day, the second day of Christmas. He died less than four months after his 70th birthday, almost exactly the same age as our father when he died. My brother was born on Labor Day and died on Boxing Day. We will have to work on the significance of all that. Boxing Day is traditionally the day after Christmas when servants in English households receive a gift from their employer in a "box," and of course Labor Day honors those who are working and gives them an extra day of rest. I do know Jim loved Christmas. My brother also died on the day our church calendar honors Stephen, the first deacon and martyr. I don't know about a martyr, but my brother was definitely a survivor. He had open-heart surgery, three cancers and at least three strokes. I did something I have never done before shortly after my brother died. I prayed asking him what he would like for us to say about him. I have given homilies at many funerals but never have prayed that question to the person who has died. I now wish I had. This is what immediately came to me that my brother said: "I tried to be a good man, and I loved my family." "I tried to be a good man, and I loved my family." So that is my message from my brother. I know he dearly loved his family and was very proud of each of his sons, Joel, Todd, and Andy and their wives Karyn, Emily, and Adrienne and their families. I know he loved Cece and his grandchildren Vie and Jack and our cousins Steve and Janie and Liz and Charlie and my children and their children. He loved this community, serving so faithfully as a banker, a member of the Boys and Girls Club and the school board. I know he especially loved this church where he also served so faithfully. Since the Episcopal Church is a love we both shared, we talked about it often. Only once did we have the privilege of serving at an altar together. That was at our mother's funeral where we both were Eucharistic ministers serving the chalice. My brother was an eight o'clock churchgoer. They are a different breed, a little more private, a little quieter, usually a little more conservative. They get the ear of the rector after the service, as there are so few people present that early. My brother loved serving on the vestry, another rare breed. If an eight o'clocker is a lector or Eucharistic minister, they serve more often than those at the later service as my brother did. I tried to talk my brother into becoming a deacon, which I think could have happened if he had had a little more time. The church is in the genes of our family. It may come out in so many different forms, but we cannot escape it.

My brother was a believer and there is no doubt that he now lives in the resurrection, just as he experienced so many resurrections in this life. What is life like in the resurrection, life with the Good Shepherd? I have no idea and I have learned to beware of people who tell us what it is like. Our only real model is Jesus, the Good Shepherd. After the resurrection Jesus is the same and different. The Good Shepherd walks through locked doors but still eats fish. He still has his wounds on his feet and hands and side, but they are healing enough so that he can walk. The Good Shepherd suddenly appears and then without notice disappears as he did on the road to Emmaus. Sometimes people who know Jesus so well like Mary Magdalene do not recognize him at first.

We can only imagine what this new life is like for my brother. I imagine seeing my brother with that amazing cherub like smile when he finds his best friend Roderick who died almost 50 years before him, and when he meets Liz's brother Tommy. Our daughter, Joanna, sent me a text when she heard my brother had died saying she was cleaning her house and crying and listening to Elvis music. Yes, I know my brother will be overcome by meeting Jesus face to face, but I have no doubt that his next words will be asking Jesus about "The King." We will all remember hearing my brother singing Elvis' favorites at Karaoke. A secret that few know is that as a child he was a boy soprano and sang solos in churches especially at Christmas. He sang the Italian Christmas Carol, *Gesu Bambino,* the best. All of my children had a special love for my brother and always ask about him.

I imagine that my brother's body is restored and renewed and he is again strong and that he is that jovial, good-humored positive self again, just waiting to help someone else out. If there are cars or silver or shoes in the resurrected life, I know he is polishing them. If there is a wide screen TV in the resurrected life, I know my brother will be there watching golf or football or basketball or better yet he now may be able to get the best seats and to go to every NC State game, but I am wondering if they allow you to wear red in the life after death.

People often ask how to work through the death of someone you love. My experience is to do something to honor their life and your relationship with them. The brother I want to remember is the one who loved life and enjoyed life and loved serving others. Perhaps that is what I want to remember, to love life and enjoy each moment and serve others. This is a gift; it was his gift. I will always especially remember that my brother was the only one present with our mother when she died. He also cared for our Aunt Rosie until she was in her 90's. That was servant ministry. Perhaps in some way we will honor my brother by serving others, and also remembering to love life.

My image of the resurrected life is that the people there who love us are constantly praying for us. Also those in the resurrection can now be with us always, as before when they were alive, they were only with us when they were physically present. The God of my understanding does not give us a relationship with someone who cares about us and loves us and then abruptly stops it. The death of someone you love is not like a period at the end of a sentence but more like a comma, where the relationship continues but in a different way. I know our parents and our grandparents so loved my brother. I am sometimes more acutely aware of the presence of my grandparents, my husband's parents, almost like angels keeping me from harm and allowing me to do things I know I would not be able to do for myself. Be aware that you too may feel my brother's prayers and his presence and his love even more than you knew when he was alive with you. As I look out and see each of you who loved my brother and Cece so much, my prayer is that we will all try to keep and hold on to all the memories of Jim that tell us that "he tried to be a good man, and he loved his family."

Walking the Mourner's Path Sermon
Martha, Mary, and Lazarus

John 11:21–27
St. Luke's • June 12, 2014

Anita and Linda and I cannot tell you what a privilege it has been to be these last eight weeks with these very brave ten women. How brave are they? Let me tell you. I cannot count the number of people or their therapists or their relatives I have talked with over the phone during this past year who had had a significant death in their life and wanted to come to Mourner's Path, who later decided they could not come: not the right time, could we change the time, worried it might be too religious, not religious enough, lived too far away, lived too close, it lasted too long, didn't last long enough, decided to grieve privately. Two weeks before we started, we had fourteen participants. A week before, it became thirteen, the first night one person never showed up or answered calls, one person left after the first night, and another sweet and hurting woman left after three nights, and so tonight we are ten. Why is this? Grief work is work, painful, like surgery and the recovery time can be just as painful. We are not always in the right place to do the work, but here they are, ten amazingly brave women who took the plunge and came to what the Celts call a thin place without the intrusions of daily life where they were able to grieve and cry and moan and laugh together, supporting each other. They immediately learned that they were in the sacred place with people who had some idea of the pain they were experiencing. I must insert that in our fifteen years of doing Mourner's Path here in Arkansas, this is the first group where we ran out of Kleenex. We did share many tears together. Stephanie has also coined a new term to describe Mourner's path, "oddly comforting."

We were all like Jesus in the garden of Gethsemane, hoping that this cup would pass, but it didn't. We did pray at the beginning and end of each session, but perhaps not as much as some thought we should. But we were in the garden of Gethsemane where Jesus said to his disciples, "sit here for awhile while I pray." He said, "While I pray." We did not have to pray. We were being prayed for by the Christ who knew we were in this garden/ and by these amazing prayer partners who held us up daily, hourly in prayer, all of which also have experienced a night in the garden. We all, like Jacob in the Old Testament, have also wrestled with God in the night. Like Jacob, we are learning that we will also walk with a limp the rest of our life. If we look carefully, we will see that the limp we each have will become very similar. We are learning and accepting that grief continues, but it does change, it morphs, even softens, but will most probably stay with us to the end.

We have talked about dreams and how our loved ones appear in dreams, not always ours, often other's dreams. We have talked about jewelry, how rubbing the piece between our fingers transports us to our loved one. We have talked of how difficult it is to lose a spouse. The vow "till death do you part" is wrong. You don't part at death. The other person does not leave you suddenly; they are in your blood, your soul, and your tissue, embroidered on your fabric. You have cell memory of your spouse. It is the same when we lose a son, a daughter, a mother. It would not be so hard if there had not been so many good times or unresolved times. People we love who die don't just leave when they die; they don't leave at all. Their essence is like a vine, still entwined around us. We carry their soul intimately with ours. They live through us, through others, not just through a memory, but becoming a part of the people they leave behind: woven fabric, fibers of steel, foundations and essence. But speaking through the soul of the living is not enough. There is resurrection.

We have been like Mary and Martha in our gospel story today. We did not think our loved one would die, or at least, not just when they did.[1] We were surprised to find out that the one we loved had died. Like Mary and Martha we have asked where was Jesus, where was God? Clouds seem to hide God from view. Why did Jesus not come and save our loved one? Perhaps we remembered that Jesus sobbed, wept, just as we did at the death of the one he loved. But this is not enough. We want to refuse death its due, and that is Jesus' example and promise for us. We know it is not enough to comfort those of us whose life has been occluded by the canopy of death with the simple temporal promise that God never leaves or forsakes us, that God is with us now, even at this horrible moment, that God wants to hold our hand. We don't want to hold God's hand, thank you very much. We want to hold our loved one's hand. We want to know that death has not won, that this god-awful and hopeless darkness is not for eternity, and that we can hope in a tomorrow. While we wait, we think of ways to honor our loved one, making albums and pictures for others and ourselves to remember them, ministering and cooking for others who are grieving, sharing their pottery and other works of art, teaching art to under privileged children. We want to believe that there is a powerful Messiah, the One who, for all time, beats death at its game on the cross and at the tomb, the one who calls Lazarus forth by his name from his grave, the one who person by person calls each of us and our loved ones by name. "I am the resurrection and the life. He who comes to me shall never die." Jesus is alive. So are our loved ones. Alive! We do not know where or how, but because Jesus is alive, we know they are as well. Death's victory is an illusion, its only grip being fear. We grieve, but we do not need to fear. We can live with confidence. Because of the God of Grace. Jesus at the grave, calls Lazarus' name. He calls our loved ones names. "Come forth," he says, "unbind them."

The ones we love who have died are in a new life, just as each of us who love them are also today because of each of you beginning a new life.

1. Rob Gieselmann, *A Walk through the Churchyard: Toward a Spirituality of Christian Death,* pp. 79–84.

INTERPRETING CHILDREN

Children Meeting God
Children's Chapel Earth Day Easter 2 B

John 20: 19–31
Cathedral School • April 22, 2009

The disciples tell Thomas, "We have seen the Lord."

What does it mean to see God? Do you think you still can see Jesus just as the disciples did on that evening after the Resurrection. Let me tell you a story about two people today who saw God.

There once was a little boy who wanted to meet God. He knew it was a long trip to where God lived, so he packed his suitcase with Twinkies and a six-pack of root beer, and he started his journey. (What would you take on your trip if you were going to see God?)

When he had gone about three blocks, he met an old woman. She was sitting in the park just staring at some pigeons. The boy sat down next to her and opened his suitcase. He was about to take a drink from his root beer when he noticed that the old lady looked hungry, so he offered her a Twinkie. She gratefully accepted it and smiled at him. Her smile was so pretty that the boy wanted to see it again, so he offered her a root beer. Once again, she smiled at him. The boy was delighted! They sat there all afternoon eating and smiling, but they never said a word. As it grew dark, the boy realized how tired he was and so he got up to leave, but before he had gone more than a few steps; he turned around, ran back to the old woman, and gave her a big hug. She gave him her biggest smile ever.

When the boy opened the door to his own house a short time later; his mother was surprised by the look of joy on his face. She asked him, "What did you do today that made you so happy?"

He replied, "I had lunch with God." But before his mother could respond, he added, "You know what? She's got the most beautiful smile I have ever seen! God has the most beautiful smile I have ever seen."

Meanwhile, the old woman, also radiant with joy, returned to her home. Her son was stunned by the look of peace on her face and he asked, "Mother, what did you do today that made you so happy?" She replied, "I ate Twinkies in the park with God." But before her son responded, she added, "You know, God is much younger than I expected . . . God is much younger than I expected."

Today Jesus is asking us to look for him in places we least expect. . where we never think we will find him. We are also being asked to be Jesus to each person we meet on our journey to see God. And I am asking you today to go out from this place, be Jesus to the people in your family and school and community . . . and look for Jesus in people you least expect. . and come back and tell us all about it just as the little boy and old woman did. That is what Jesus is calling us today to do . . . to share our Jesus stories with each other just as the disciples, John, and Thomas have shared their stories with us today.

Story given to me by storyteller, Jerre Roberts from Texarkana.

Carry Your Light

Children's Sermons Chapel
Cathedral School, 2009

Once there was a Jewish congregation that did not have their own synagogue. For many years they had met together in other buildings saving and planning for the day when they might have a place to call their own. Finally the day arrived when they decided they had enough money to hire an architect and begin construction of their dream.

They interviewed a number of prospective architects. Some of them only wanted to talk about what they felt the new building should be like. Others listened for a while but rapidly returned to describing their own plans and ideas. There was one architect though that was unlike all the others. He listened for a very long time. He asked them what their dreams were for this new building. When the time to hire the architect came he was the choice of all the people. They felt he was the only one who understood their vision for what this building could be for the community.

When they offered him the contract he said, "I am honored that you have chosen me. But you must understand that I do not work like other architects. I will not submit a design to you nor will you see the building until it is completed. I will continue to listen to you through the suggestion box I will put up and I will give my attention to everything that is put there."

This took the people aback. They were hesitant to go forward with no concrete plans but at the same time they felt that he was the only one who listened to and understood their dreams. So they hired him.

Immediately the suggestion box was filled with ideas. In the beginning he had to empty it twice—sometimes even three times a week. Even after ground was broken and construction began-concealed from them in some way they did not understand—still people wrote down their latest thoughts and ideas for the architect. Always, the box was emptied promptly.

After some time, the architect came back to the people and told them that the building was completed and that he would reveal it to them late in the afternoon of the following Thursday.

Well before the appointed hour people began to gather at the site. The air was filled with anticipation. They wondered to themselves and aloud to each other if their ideas would have found a place in the completed building. They walked all around the site imagining what it might be like. Finally at 4 p.m. the architect appeared before them welcoming them and somehow lifting the veil that had concealed the building from their view.

A great cheer arose. As they looked at the building each person felt that it was exactly as he had hoped it might be. Each person felt that the architect had not only followed the words they had written but had somehow known what was in their hearts. Together they circled the building.

Then the architect opened the great doors and welcomed them in. They explored every part of the building coming finally to gather together in the sanctuary. They walked around examining everything and finally each found a place to sit. It was beginning to get dark and someone went to switch on the lights. To his amazement no light switches could be found. Then they examined the walls and found there were no outlets there. They all turned to the architect and said, "How could you build us this perfect building without any lights."

"Oh," said the architect, "there are lights. Come." He led them to the back of the sanctuary and opened the doors to a great cupboard. he began to pull out small lamps by tens and finally by hundreds. He passed the lamps out until each person had one. "Look here," the architect said. He pointed out hundreds of small hooks on the walls all around the room that no one had noticed before.

"When you leave tonight," he said. "Take your lamp with you. Carry it with you when you return. Light it and hang it on the wall near where you sit. If you are not here your place will remain dark. For no one can carry your light but you."

Story given to me by storyteller, Jerre Roberts from Texarkana.

A Visit from St. Nikolas
to the Advent Eucharist at Cathedral School

Trinity Cathedral, Little Rock • December 1, 2010

Today we are celebrating the feast day of St. Nikolas and I think St. Nikolas is actually coming to visit us today.

Do you hear him? *Knock, Knock.*

Welcome, welcome St. Nikolas. Do you know these amazing children who attend The Cathedral School?

Are you speaking Greek?

We know you are a Greek bishop, from Myra. I believe that is on the southern coast of Turkey. I know a little Greek. Do you know any English?

No, all right I will translate your answers to the children.

You say you are a Greek saint and lived in the 300's, the third century so you do not know any English. Are you up to answering some questions about yourself, for there are so many rumors and stories about you that we are having a hard time knowing what is really the truth?

The children would like to know about your parents.

Your parents were very rich and were Christians, but died when you were young, a teenager. When they died you went to live in a monastery with your uncle, also named Nickolas who was the abbot there. When you inherited their money, you gave all of it to the poor and those in need especially other children.[1]

You were made a bishop and later you were put in prison because you were a Christian. You attended the Council of Nicea. Oh, yes, we have heard of that council. That is where we get the Nicean creed that we say on Sundays, and you were there! Amazing!

The children want to know how you became a bishop?

A very long time ago, when the Bishop of Myra died, the other bishops in Lycia gathered to select the new bishop for Myra. As they met, they discussed and prayed, but could not discern who would be the right choice. One night, the oldest and wisest bishop heard a voice in the night telling him to watch the doors of the church the next morning before morning prayers. The first person to enter the church by the name of "Nicholas" was to be the new bishop. This wise bishop shared his vision with the others, urging them to pray while he waited at the doors. And the next morning you went to Morning Prayer as you usually did and so became a bishop.

Tell us how you became noted for gift giving.

There was a poor man with three daughters.[1] In those days a young woman's father had to offer prospective husbands something of value—a dowry. The larger the dowry, the better the chance that a young woman would find a good husband. Without a dowry, a woman was unlikely to marry. This poor man's daughters, without dowries, were now destined to be sold into slavery. Mysteriously, on three different occasions, you put a bag of gold in their home-providing the needed dowries. The bags of gold, tossed through an open window, are said to have landed in their stockings or shoes left before the fire to dry. This led to the custom of children hanging stockings or putting out shoes, eagerly awaiting gifts from St. Nikolas (that's you). Sometimes the story is told with gold balls instead of bags of gold. That is why three gold balls, sometimes represented as oranges, are one of the symbols for St. Nicholas. And so you are known as a gift-giver.

We hear you are also a protector of sailors and your prayers have saved them when they were at sea.

Bishop Nikolas, do you have any idea how you got mixed up with Santa Claus?

It is a mystery. Some believe the Dutch colonist brought you here, for they called you *Sinterklass*,[2] that soon became Santa Claus in America, but this is still a great mystery.

St. Nikolas, since this is your feast day and you are a Greek bishop, can you teach us a little Greek?

"Thank you" in Greek is pronounced "Efxaristo" emphasizing the final "o." In Greek it is written "Ευχαριστώ."

It means Thank you!

You are teaching us to say thank you for the gifts we receive especially on your feast day.

This looks like the word we use in our language for Eucharist. You are telling us that the word for Eucharist is from the Greek and means, *thank you*, so when we have the Eucharist, which we will soon be doing at the table, it is really a thank you.

I also heard that you have a gift for each child as they are leaving today. So for today when we receive your gift, we will try to say, "Ευχαριστώ."

As for now we want to say thank you, "Ευχαριστώ," for taking time to visit with us on your special day!

1. "Who is St. Nicholas?", St. Nicholas Center, Discovering the Truth about Santa Claus, www.stnicholascenter.org

2. "Saint Nicholas," Wikipedia, en.wikipedia.org/wki/Saint_Nicholas.

St. Nikolas. *Photograph by Joanna Seibert.*

INTERPRETING DISASTER

17A Take up your cross

Matthew 16:21–28
St. Luke's • August 31, 2014

"If any want to become my followers, let them deny themselves and take up their cross and follow me."

15 years ago this summer Wednesday, June 2, 1999.[1,2,3]

All of Little Rock mourns the crash last night of American Flight 1420 from Dallas at the Little Rock airport. During a severe thunderstorm shortly before midnight Tuesday, the aircraft skids off the end of runway 4R, crashes into a bank of landing lights and a metal tower and lands in a flood plain of the Arkansas River 15 feet below the runway. The steel poles act like a can opener, peeling back the plane's thin shell on its left side, from the captain's controls through the first-class section. Fire engulfs the plane as fuel spills.

The captain and eight passengers have died so far. Five of the dead are from Russellville, one from Havana, Arkansas, and one from Paragould. Throughout the day Arkansans relive the times they were on that same last flight from Dallas to Little Rock.

One of the dead is Sue Gray, a retired Russellville schoolteacher. Gray, 78, was always doing something at All Saints Episcopal Church—working the flower garden, teaching Sunday school, embroidering altar linens. She had been on a two-week tour of Britain.

Images of the disabled plane speak to the miracle of the 129 survivors, mostly Arkansans. They are the first to survive a U.S. commercial airplane crash since 1994. Conversations in this capitol city center around eye witness accounts from survivors. The stories are a spectrum of human behavior. One of the first and most haunting reports is by Little Rock native Carla Koen at Children's Hospital Burn Unit. As she tries to escape from the burning plane through the hole in its side, she is caught on the jagged edges and becomes trapped hanging by one leg upside down. Other passengers spill out over and on top of her, scrambling to get out. "They poured over me while I was hanging there, but no one stopped to help me," she cries. "One angry, panicked man even screamed at me as I dangled upside down for me to move and get out of his way so he could get out of the wreckage. I'll see his face for the rest of my life," responds this survivor.

I as well have been haunted for years by this man. Would I have stopped to help Carla Koen or would I have trampled over her in my panic for safety from the burning plane? I know how I hope I would have acted, but I can't be sure. When Carla Koen finally frees her leg and jumps to safety, she soon is caring for two young girls alone and terrified in the adjacent hay field in the driving rain and hail. Erin and Cara Ashcraft, 13 and 10, are on the flight to visit their grandparents in Arkansas. Koen stays with the girls and tries to divert their attention from the disaster, asking where they are from (Flower Mound, Texas), and if the have any pets (yes, a poodle) and if they play any musical instruments (Erin plays the clarinet). Koen comforts Erin who is distraught because her hair, singed by the fire, is falling out in chucks. "I tried to talk to them about life and how we were alive and that was the most important thing," Koen says, adding that the girls helped her as well. "They gave me something else to focus on." She doesn't allow the lack of consideration to help her become a "stumbling block," an obsession, that could keep her from reaching out to others.

"If any want to become my followers, let them deny themselves and take up their cross and follow me."

More stories surface about 25 members of the Ouachita Baptist University choir returning from a two-week European tour where they had entertained Kosovo refugees in Austria. In the chaos that follows the crash, the singers work again as a team. Barrett Barber, a 19-year-old minister's son, lifts passengers through a hole in the plane above an emergency exit that would not open. Choir member Luke Hollingsworth escapes from the tail section only to go back to help wounded passengers escape. On his own shoulders, the young man carries a woman with a broken pelvis across chest-deep water to safety. Choir director Charles Fuller gets his wife out then goes back into the burning plane to help rescue an 80-year-old man with a broken hip. He is later seen guiding other passengers out of the fuselage onto the wing of the plane.

The acts of heroism don't end even after the young people have gotten survivors off the plane. Rain and huge balls of hail are pelting down on injured passengers lying on the ground. Choir members huddle over them, using their own bodies as human shields against the hail and rain. Young men take off their shirts to form makeshift blankets for the injured. When a physician arrives at the crash site, he tells reporters he is "amazed at the calmness and stoicism that I witnessed."

"If any want to become my followers, let them deny themselves and take up their cross and follow me."

The heroism does not come without a price. Choir member James Harrison repeatedly runs back into the burning plane to pull passengers to safety. He is overcome by smoke, collapses, and dies. One of the young girls saved by James Harrison also later dies at Children's Hospital. Rachel Fuller, Harrison's choir leader's daughter, is fourteen, a 4.0 honor student and oboe player from Arkadelphia.

10 years ago, June 2004.[4]

It is 5 years after the crash at the dedication of a memorial to honor heroes of flight 1420.

Comments from survivors:

"Having a life and not wasting a day is what this is all about," says survivor Kelly Williams. Sharon Agnleman, 43, no longer wears a watch. 69 year old Little Rock native, Nancy Wood says, "We live each day to the fullest." Vocalist Kristen Maddox was an operatic singer before the crash, but smoke inhalation severely damaged her voice. Her hands were also critically burned. She finds a new life, graduating from nursing school the month before the memorial. She believes that she was led to this new vocation by the compassionate care she received during her many arduous hospital stays.

"Take up your cross and follow me. For those who want to save their life will lose it, and those who lose their life for my sake will find it."

July 2009. Ten years after the crash.

The Ouachita singers meet to remember the two of their singers who died, Rachel Fuller and James Harrison, and sing the songs that made them a community. Their choir director Charles Fuller talked about how music has the power to touch and heal hearts.

Is Jesus calling us today to give up our life as James Harrison and Rachael Fuller did? The chances of our ever being in a plane crash are unbelievably slim: 1 in 11 million. We do sometimes meet situations that seem like an airline disas-

74

ter. A friend or family member dies. We or a family member or a friend develops cancer. Our children get into trouble. We lose our job. We cannot meet the house payments. Our spouse leaves us. Our children move away. There is no question that we have been given a cross to bear and it is very heavy and we see no Simon of Cyrene around to carry it for us. We feel like Carla Koen, hanging by one leg up side down dangling out of a burning airplane.

There is more to this gospel than about cross bearing and dying. The disciples missed the message and we often do as well. "And on the third day you will be raised." We know this is true in the life to come, but does the blessing the resurrection occur today, right now for the cross bearing we are doing today? Resurrection and blessing are written all over flight 1420. Kristin Maddox looses her voice, her career, but sees through her pain and suffering another opportunity to serve as a nurse. Nancy Wood, Kelly Williams, and Sharon Agnleman learn what is really important in life, living one day at a time.

Today 15 years later if you attend a performance of the Arkansas Symphony this fall at Maumelle High School, you will see that the oboe principal chair is a memorial to Rachel Fuller. If you go to the burn unit at Children's Hospital you will learn that the doctor there is being supported by an endowed chair in burn treatment given by Rachel's parents, Cindy and Charles Fuller.

My prayers are that if called to do so, I might become a James Harrison and give up my life for others. But my ability to do this is still in doubt. More realistically I pray that I can be a Carla Koen. When I feel as if I am hanging by one leg upside down in a burning disaster, my experience tells me, that I will survive. And when I get back on my feet, instead of harboring resentment for the situation and for the people who were not helpful, I pray I can reach out to serve others in similar circumstances. My experience tells me this is the only way healing occurs. Another name for this is blessing and resurrection.

Note from Pat Wiggins, another passenger, whom we met at Bravo Restaurant by chance at lunch after giving this sermon:

"Thank you so much for sharing! It really was serendipity, wasn't it?! Also wanted to tell you that I was seated on the plane next to Barrett Barber and that James Harrison reportedly died at my seat (according to Andrea Harter). I was seated in the back with the choir

members because I had taken a "bump" that morning at LAX to get a bigger (and I thought safer) plane from Dallas to LR. My luggage arrived safely in LR on the small plane, late that Tues. afternoon."

1. Linda S. Caillouet, "Fleeing survivors trod on entangled woman," *Arkansas Democrat-Gazette,* Thursday, June 3, 1999.

2. Joanna Seibert, "Flight 1420, A Community of Survivors and Servants," *The Living Church,* July 11, 1999.

3. Andrea Harter, "Surviving 1420," a four-part series, *Arkansas Democrat-Gazette,* January 23–26, 2000.

4. Andrea Harter, "Flight 1420 survivors to gather, crash memorial dedication today," *Arkansas Democrat-Gazette,* Tuesday June 1, 2004.

Hurricane Katrina

Romans 12:9–21
Trinity Cathedral • September 4, 2005

Eight months ago, as we celebrated the twelve days of Christmas, we watched in horror the tsunami disaster half a world away. This week before Labor Day a "tsunami-like" hurricane takes place in our own backyard. All week we have been glued to our television screens to hear the latest media reports from our neighboring states of Louisiana and Mississippi and Alabama of a disaster of unbelievable proportions. Part of our own country now looks like something from the apocalypse, a doom's day movie, a scene only played out in a third world country . . . bodies floating on main street, hospitals where the highest level of care is taking vital signs, 80% of one of our nearest and favorite cities under water (Canal Street literally becoming a canal again). Thousands of people in New Orleans and the Mississippi gulf coast weather the storm but now are without home, food, water, communications, electricity. They frantically wave clothes from their rooftops after they have crawled through holes in their attics to freedom. There is ruthless looting, people walking the streets with shotguns on their shoulders. Gunshots are heard throughout the city.

There seem to be two groups of people in incredible need, those still stranded in New Orleans and the gulf coast/ and those who left before the hurricane now unable to go home. Over a million people evacuated their homes and are now displaced persons who do not know what will be there or when they can return home. Meanwhile where do they go, where do they stay? Even closer to home we hear from the bishops of Mississippi and Louisiana that six Episcopal Churches have been totally destroyed in Mississippi with serious damage to many others. At least 18 church buildings in Louisiana have disappeared. The diocesan office in Louisiana floods on Thursday, but it had already been looted the day before.

We intently hear Paul's words to the Romans today: "Let love be genuine; hate what is evil, hold fast to what is good; love one another with mutual affection; outdo one another in showing honor. Do not lag in zeal, be ardent in spirit, serve the Lord. Rejoice in hope, be patient in suffering, persevere in prayer. Contribute to the needs of the saints; extend hospitality to strangers."

YES, YES, YES, LORD . . . we really want to do all this. We see our brother and sister hurting . . . What can we do , . . right now! Today. Yesterday! We wish we could be superman, find a phone booth, go into it, change our clothes, come out and fly down to the coast, blow away all the water, rescue victims, clean up and restore the tall buildings, homes, lives, churches with a single bound. If only we could be coast guard helicopter pilots and circle the city by day and night to rescue those still trapped in their homes. If only we could be members of the transport team of our own Children's Hospital who have been in New Orleans this past week transporting children to surrounding hospitals. If only we could be the cardiologist and a respiratory therapist flying to New Orleans to rescue a gravely ill 15-year -old boy waiting for a heart transplant. He is on ventricular assist and the electricity is out. They resuscitate him as they carry him down two flights of stairs in the darkness to a waiting pick up truck, which takes him to the adjacent parking lot roof where they fly him to Texas Children's. They will go to their grave remembering this teenaged boy who is conscious the whole trip and is constantly thanking them for saving his life. If only we were trained to do something like that. Helping those who are still trapped by the storm.

What about those who have left their homes and become like wandering Aramaeans. We hear from Gene Crawford, our deacon in south Arkansas: "Our small town of Crossett currently has an estimated 200 people displaced by Hurricane Katrina. Our hotels are full and members of our community have opened their homes to those who have arrived and, yes, continue to arrive. Today we began serving meals at First Baptist Church. I attend a meeting at the Chamber— a gathering of ministers, concerned citizens, and civic leaders who last week were at odds with each other over multiple issues. In one hour we put aside all our differences and put together our response to those in need: housing, food, child care, money vouchers, clothes." Should we travel down to Crossett and help them out? They seem to have it all together.

Soon we learn we can send money to our diocese for Katrina relief, to the Red Cross, to the Episcopal Relief and Development Fund. We can do this. We learn in our weekly newsletter and a special communication from the dean that we can bring items here to Trinity, which will be taken to the gulf coast. We can do that. We can "contribute to the needs of the saints," those suffering this disaster.

The people of the gulf coast and New Orleans ask for our prayers. Oh, yes. We can offer our prayers. Yes, we can "persevere in prayer."

But, if only we could go to the coast, do something, move trees, sweep, hand out water and food, sit and listen to people tell their stories, but access is impossible. It is a dangerous place to be. It is a war zone. Few are getting in. How do we personally "extend hospitality to strangers?" I sit watching television and surfing the Internet paralyzed by the magnitude of the need and feeling so inadequate. Then I remember some advice from a friend who was also paralyzed by the magnitude of the problems in her life. She became even more overwhelmed one Monday morning, which in a former era used to be "wash day," (do you remember) Monday, the only day we all washed our dirty clothes. She went to her laundry room and looked at the floor piled ceiling high with dirty clothes. She sat down and cried. "I can not do this. The job is overwhelming. I don't know where to start!"

Then insight came. "Yes, you can. You can do this: you wash one load at a time." One load at a time.

And this was Jesus' example to us . . . one job, one healing, one person at a time. He ministered to one person at a time . . . and this is what our Lord calls us to do. We are not called to minister to the millions devastated by this hurricane . . . but to one person we meet, one person at a time.

It takes me the whole week to remember Jesus' one on one ministry. I am taught this by members of my family and this congregation who visit shelters and hotels here in Little Rock where people from Louisiana have come to seek refugee.

Perhaps we will eventually be able to go to New Orleans or the gulf coast or even Crossett. But there are families in need literally in our backyard. As you well know, hundreds and soon thousands of the one million people who left New Orleans will be right here in Little Rock. How do we reach them? Canon Wheatley and Dean Hudson have been closely involved in organizing help for families who have come to Little Rock and they soon will be telling us how we can help. Plans are being made to open Camp Mitchell to evacuees and our help will be needed there.

But let me tell you about just one person. Shannon lives in Little Rock. She has a new baby and two small children under five, and like the rest of us, her heart aches for those displaced from their homes. While I am still glued to the television and my computer, she instead goes to a hotel a few blocks from her house where she hears people from New Orleans are staying. She just sits in the hotel lobby in the morning with her 4-month-old baby while her other two children are in school. People come up to her and ask where in Louisiana is she from? When they find out she is local, they pour their heart out to her. She learns what everyone else from Crossett and all who have gone to shelters have told us. People desperately need to tell someone their story of what has happened to them. She talks with three families. They all had multiple family members, parents, grandparents, children and pets trying to stay together. She then goes back home to her computer, to the Red Cross, gets numbers for them to call about specific needs, connects them to medical care, housing and schools for their children. But mostly she gives her PRESENCE.

This week I learn from you and young people like Shannon that ministry need never be in a distant place. We do not have to go to Biloxi or New Orleans or even Crossett. We just walk out our front door and go a few blocks to fulfill Paul's call to the Romans and to us: "to serve the Lord, to rejoice in hope, to contribute to the needs of the saints; to extend hospitality to strangers."

And finally, one more question. Where in the world is our God, the one who is petitioning us to "hold fast to what is good and be patient in suffering"? Where has this God been, who is asking us "to rejoice in hope and extend hospitality to strangers?"

I think all of us have seen thousands of pictures of our God this week. Since Monday we have been at the foot of the cross watching a scene from GOOD FRIDAY. Ours is a God/ who SUFFERS for us and with us. Our God is sitting on the roof of his floating home waving a torn white shirt. Our God just barely survived the

The Gulf Coast Oil Spill 2010—tar balls.
Photograph by Joanna Seibert.

horrors of the New Orleans Convention Center and now is on a bus to Arkansas. Our God is in a bed/ in the dark at Charity Hospital New Orleans. Our God is sitting this morning with hands lifted up in the midst of the remains of St. Peter's and St. Mark's, Gulfport. Our God will soon be walking into Camp Mitchell owning only the clothes on his back. Our God is living at the Baymont Inn in Little Rock trying to hold his family together . . . and today our God asks us TO MEET HIM THERE, TO BECOME A WITNESS TO HIS RESURRECTION.

28C The Gulf Coast Oil Spill 2010

Luke 21: 5–19
Trinity Cathedral

"And there will be great earthquakes . . . dreadful portents
and great signs from heaven."

Chapter 1

It is mid August, still the height of the summer tourist season on the Alabama gulf coast. We arrive at the condominium that has been our family's vacation home for twenty-five years. Ours is the only car in the parking lot. Beyond our balcony on the fourth floor, the blue green gulf is calm, a cool breeze blows to the east, but only a few isolated sunbathers lie on the white sandy beaches. Double red flags are flying. No bathers are swimming. At dusk arrive a covey of beach buggies called UTVs motoring up and down the beach followed by shiny green tractors pulling covered trailers with benches on either side for beach cleanup workers wearing colored shirts. The color of their shirt is like a liturgical vestment (dalmatic or chasuble) signifying the duty of the worker. The UTVs and John Deere tractors and trailers carry ice chests, tents, lights, and portapoties. One UTV stops near our condominium. Two workers get out and look at the sand near the surf. A half hour later a new John Deere tractor slowly pulls a trailer with workers. They set up a blue tent and folding chairs. The workers sift the sand for 20 minutes and then rest under the tent. Later comes a lone person walking slowly like a verger or crucifer in a religious procession striding in front of a UTV followed by a green tractor pulling a large machine that rakes the sand. At night the tractor pulling the sand sifting machine has two large lights on either side like processional torches. The processional leader is trained to look for alternating or simultaneous right and left flipper turtle tracks in the sand leading to a loggerhead sea turtle nest that should not be disturbed by the mechanical beach rake. We see few pelicans, no Great Blue Herons, no dolphins. Only the laughing gulls are unchanged in numbers and squawking. No fishing boats leave the pass to venture into the gulf for the catch of the day. Hidden under the Perdido Pass Bridge are large white tents as you might see at a revival or the circus. The area is chained off with guards at the entrance. At a local restaurant we have no difficulty finding our favorite seat. Most locals report their businesses falling off 30 to 60%. The worst hit are the commercial and charter fishermen and shrimpers who have completely lost their business. From the window of a favorite restaurant by a marina we watch charter fishermen hosing down their boats like boys on a Saturday afternoon washing their cars in expectation for that Saturday night date. For the fishermen the date does not materialize. Members of our family grieve for one charter boat captain who frequently took them out to fish. He has committed suicide. Henry's, the local furniture store is going out of business. Only Henry is there answering the phone, showing off the little stock left, and taking last minute orders. Nearly 185 million gallons of oil have violated the gulf since the explosion on the oilrig on April 20th of this year that also killed eleven workers. In the twenty-five years we have been part of the community of the gulf coast, we have survived with them minor and major hurricanes such as Ivan and Katrina. This disaster, however, has so many more unknowns and long reaching effects.

"You will be betrayed even by parents and brothers, by relatives and friends. But not a hair of your head will perish. By your endurance you will gain your souls."

Chapter 2

One month later the oil well is permanently capped. We return to Paradise Island as the locals call it. The parking lot is now three quarters full. We sit on our balcony watching the early dawn turn light then pink then orange. At daybreak three men and three children come to the surf and cast their lines for early morning breakfast. They are simultaneously joined by five Great Blue Herons stalking behind them, craning their long necks, observing every movement of the fishing lines, hoping for a free meal. I cannot hold back tears as we watch small and large fishing boats leave the pass in the early morning to go to unknown parts of the gulf for more hidden treasures of the sea. A single red flag is flying, but there are now bathers venturing in and out of the surf at the water's edge. My husband only finds two small tar balls on his morning walk. No workers patrol the beaches during the day. Their guarded headquarters under the Perdido Pass Bridge is almost deserted.

Flocks of pelicans fly by. Dolphins glide by in parade and occasionally jump for joy. We do not go early enough to our favorite restaurant to get the table with the best gulf view. Life seems to be restored. It looks like resurrection. We go in the afternoon to a Eucharist and healing service at a local church to give thanksgiving. People come to the altar rail for healing. As members of the congregation, their priest, and I place our hands on them, they pray through their tears for strength to meet the financial and personal losses they have endured. During the Eucharist we hear a dog barking. At the peace a member of the congregation goes out to find a gray dog with matted hair in its kennel abandoned at the church door. The priest, Chris, interrupts the service and Chan goes out to give the dog water. Another parishioner plans to take the dog to a friend who "needs a dog." Someone can no longer care for a special member of the family so leaves it with another family they hope will care. Later at the vet's, the parishioner and the dog, now named Rags, find out this is a pure bred Lhaso Apso, probably a year old. This breed originated in Tibet and was bred primarily as interior guard dogs for Buddhist monasteries and palaces. It was thought that the souls of the lamas entered the Lhaso Apso while awaiting reincarnation.

We see scars that will be with this community for years to come, but we learn a great deal about what a house of God can be. . a place for people in great distress to go for healing in community, to share their pain and be surrounded and touched by the many hands of God.

Back at the condo we read in the paper that a federal survey of the Florida, Alabama, and Mississippi coast finds tar balls still washing ashore with every wave and bands of oil buried under 4 or 5 inches of clean sand. The Old Bay Steamer in downtown Fairhope, a favorite seafood restaurant for twenty-five years is closing Sunday. The owner reports that sales have bottomed out as people fear eating contaminated local seafood, especially the royal red shrimp, their specialty. Our hearts ache. We look out from our balcony for some hope.

As the bewitching hour of five o'clock approaches, nine cars pull off on the highway shoulder by our condo. Twenty people dressed in black emerge from the cars and go to the beach. There is an apparent leader, a photographer. The dress code for beach portraits must have changed from white to black. We watch for almost two hours as the family gathers in various groups for candid shots. Farther down the beach we now see a trellis covered with flowers. Four bridesmaids in red dresses arrive with the bride and groom barefoot under their white wedding garments. An ancient liturgy has returned to the beach. At dusk three people with lime green shirts walk out to a roped off area about fifty yards from our condo. They have a shovel, a bucket, a stethoscope and surgical gloves. My husband goes

Rainbow at the Gulf after a Storm. *Photograph by Joanna Seibert.*

down along with about a half dozen children on the beach to see what this "medical" team is doing. The "green" team demands that all be perfectly still. Perfectly still. A young woman with the green shirt lies on the beach and puts the stethoscope to the sand. She hears movement. They remove the wire mesh previously placed over the Loggerhead sea turtle nest to protect it from coyotes and raccoons. They gently dig into the sand with their surgical gloves, careful not to rotate and move the remaining eggs in the nest and find six newly hatched baby loggerhead turtles that have just absorbed their yolk sac. Demeter herself could not have been more motherly lifting the two and one half inch turtles to the bucket and transporting them to the shoreline. The leader in the green shirt makes a trough in the sand to the surf. The sea turtles are placed in the trench and the crowd cheers as they ceremoniously parade awkwardly to the sea. Loggerhead turtles have been nesting on beaches all over the world for over 150 million years. It takes 25 to 30 years for loggerheads to reach sexual maturity. Only one in 1000 to one in 10,000 loggerhead eggs reach adulthood. Will these six by chance be in this number?

"You will be betrayed even by parents and brothers, by relatives and friends. But not a hair of your head will perish. By your endurance you will gain your souls."

Chapter 3

What will be the future for our gulf? But it is not our gulf. We have been stewards of it now for twenty-five years. It will soon belong to our children and grandchildren. Our hope lies in today's children being photographed with their families, the young couple being married on the beach tonight, the four groomsmen and bridesmaids, the three young people fishing on the surf in the early morning and in the half dozen children who cheered the loggerhead sea turtles into the surf this magical night.

Epiphany 4A Response to Tucson Shooting

Micah 6:1–8
Trinity Cathedral • January 30, 2011

"And what does the Lord require of you but to do justice, and to love kindness, and to walk humbly with your God?"

This was the favorite Bible verse of Mrs. Horace (Mildred) Turner, my fifth grade Sunday school teacher at the West Point Methodist Church. I have been thinking of her and of this verse during the past three weeks as I have been processing the shooting in Tucson on January 8th where six people were killed including a nine-year-old third-grade budding school politician, Christina Green, born on 9/11/2001, who wanted to meet her congresswoman.[1] Twenty-two-year-old Jared Loughner opened fire on the morning crowd with a semi-automatic weapon shooting 20 people and seriously wounding congresswoman Gabrielle Giffords. As I process how we should respond to this massacre in front of a local Safeway Store, the sensing part of me researches the media and friends as to how others are reacting. FBI data reports that sales of handguns two days after the shooting jumped 60% in Tucson.[2] Arizona gun dealers attribute the spike in sales to fears that the government may crack down on gun possession in the wake of the tragedy. Others attribute the gun rush to basic fear: "Whenever there is a huge event, especially when it's close to home, people tend to run out and buy something to protect their family," says Don Gallardo, manager of Arizona Shooter's World in Phoenix. Representatives Heath Shuler of North Carolina and Jason Chaffetz of Utah announce that they will be wearing guns in their home districts. One commentator in the New York Times reminisces[3] about the 1800's when politicians regularly wore weapons on the House and Senate floor. The title of her article is "When Congress was armed and dangerous." The *Washington Post* reports that leaders of the Westboro Baptist Church of Topeka, Kansas, are planning to protest at Christina Green's funeral because "God sent the shooter to deal with idolatrous America." Obama delivers remarks at an evening memorial service at the University of Arizona, focusing on service to country and honoring the victims, especially those who were martyrs at this tragedy such as Dory

Stoddard, a fixture at the Mountain Avenue Church of Christ who died as he dived on top of his wife, Bobbie, shielding her from gunfire. Pundants argue over how present politicians that lead by fear have brought on this tragedy. Robert Wright[3] in the *New York Times* adds in our technological trends as the driver for the political leaders working out of a fear base rhetoric to portray certain Americans as evil aliens as they demonize people whose views we never see depicted by anyone other than their adversaries. Wright warns us against only viewing the world in our private cocoon of cable channels and web sites that may insulate us from the inconvenient facts.

Perhaps the most profound reaction I have heard was by Lou Ellen Treadway, a member of Trinity Cathedral. I listened to her as we sat and had breakfast on January 11th after a prayer service at Trinity before Governor Beebe's inauguration. Lou Ellen saw this tragedy as a call for us as individuals and as a country to reach out, help, and care for people with mental illness and addiction.

Indeed Robert Wright[4] writes in the *Times* about the mental status of the shooter. Jared Loughner's writings suggest that he was convinced that a conspiracy was afoot, a conspiracy by the government to control our thoughts. So he decides to kill one of the conspirators. It's pretty safe to bet that if you decide to go kill a bunch of innocent people, that you are not a picture of mental health. Now in retrospect, teachers and friends speak of Loughner's mental state and addictive life style. One of his recent teachers ordered him not to return to class until he had a mental health evaluation, which never took place. He had been barred from classes because of violent behavior.[5,6]

Charles Chatham,[7] a former priest in this diocese, describes the day after the shooting as a sad and serious Sunday.

He, like the rest of us, is disturbed about the shooting and the implications for our politics, this struggling state and our nation from here on. "What we're hoping and praying for is that we can honor the memory of those who died with some kind of rational, national self-intervention into our country's state of affairs socially, politically, spiritually and psychologically! Events like this shooting are reminiscent of the shock of President Kennedy's assassination and of the disturbing string of violence in this country in the immediate years that followed that is still a fearful and escalating reality today.

God help us all into some kind of serious personal, social, spiritual and political self-evaluation that will produce healing, not more wounding! Let us pray that this awful event shocks us into beginning a national "recovery," a movement toward a deeper and more pervasive respect for human life, human goodness. Our prayer is that this tragedy revive our global vocation especially during this Epiphany season, to be one of the "lights to the nations" rather than a growing and darkening example of how to lose national self-respect and implode as so many other nations seem to be doing year-by-year!

The Christian Church and the Episcopal Church in particular in this country were conceived in just such an environment of tragedy and fear. And from that the Episcopal Church has become respected for our rational, courageous and compassionate approach to life—spiritually, socially and politically! We have had our share of martyrs for the national causes of human rights, race relations, economics, and education. We have been respected in decades and centuries past for a thinking spirituality and biblical reasoning that combines the best of faith, intelligence and compassion. We have produced generations of thinking and faithful Christians and congregations that do not turn the lights off in our hearts and minds on Monday mornings when the last church bells ring on Sunday!

Our churches need to speak to this society today and every day that follows, to our own people about events like the Tucson violence, and get on our knees and ask for the wisdom, guidance and strength to try to turn the tide. Our Episcopal Church has been at the forefront of compassion, wisdom, peace and justice its whole history, and our members have often paid the ultimate price for their courage and faith all over this world. How can we just go to church, worship a politically executed Savior who now lives spiritually to strengthen us to make tough decisions and put our lives on the line to better this world's health and wholeness, and not respond in any other way? That's our calling, no matter who we are." That seems to have been the calling of Dory Stoddard. Hear the words of his minister at Dory's memorial service.[8] "There are no monuments to Dory, there are no streets named after him. He was just an ordinary man. He did not become a hero that day—he was a hero every day of his life."

As one theologian says[7]: our vocations are not only about religion. We have a God-given vocation in the world. That's our national vocation as citizens of this country: guided along the way by many well-known and unknown Episcopalians, people of every race, women and men, educated and not, wealthy and poor, to help create a "more just society," being remembered not by our fears and those we hate, but by how well we have loved, in the name of Jesus. Who, by the way, died trying to do the same thing in his day, and is risen and among us to make sure it's not forgotten that the whole vocation and hope never dies" that day after day, hour after hour that we "do justice, and love kindness, and walk humbly with your God!"[7]

1. James Buck, Melissa Bell, "Tucson shooting victims: lives remembered," *Washington Post,* 1/9/2011.

2. Michael Riley, "Arizona Shootings Trigger Surge in Glock Sales Amid Fear of Ban, " *Bloomberg,* January 11, 2011.

3. Joanne B. Freeman, "When Congress was Armed and Dangerous," *New York Times,* January 11, 2011.

4. Robert Wright, "First Comes Fear," *New York Times,* January 11, 2011.

5. Alexandra Berzon, John Emshwiller, Robert Guth, "Postings of a Troubled Mind, *Wall Street Journal,* January 12, 2011.

6. Jo Becker, Serge F. Kovaleski, Michael Luo, Dan Barry, "Looking Behind the Mug-Shot Grin, *New York Times,* January 15, 2011.

7. Charles Chatham, "A Sad and Serious Sunday," *Thinking Faith* #64.

8. Matthew Shaffer, "Dorwan Stoddard, RIP," *National Review Online,* January 10, 2011.

INTERPRETING MOTHER'S DAY

Mother's Left Behind
May Trinity Cathedral • Mother's Day

We are at the Bowen conference during Lent at one of our favorite retreat centers, Kanuga, in the western hills of North Carolina. Bea comes to the table and immediately we know this is a special woman. Does Bea mean beautiful? Maybe, but I think the name is short for Beatrice which means blessed. She is from Beaumont, Texas, but does not have a southern accent. She was born in Germany. Her parents were Jewish, but not practicing. She is a Holocaust survivor. She escaped from Germany, lived in Belgium and France where she was helped by the French underground. There she met her future husband, Henry Buller, a Mennonite, who was a conscientious objector doing relief work in unoccupied France and later in England and Germany. She came to this country when she was in her twenties. Is she now seventy or maybe even eighty years old? Actually she is eighty-four. She is articulate and knowledgeable and just an interesting conversationalist. She became a Mennonite but now attends a Disciples of Christ church since there is not a Mennonite congregation in her town, but she says, "I will always be a Mennonite." Kathryn comments on her unusual oriental necklace. "I do not like living alone," Bea says. "It was a gift several years ago from Chinese graduate students who lived with me." Bea notices my husband's bronze star lapel pin. She asks how he was awarded it. "I served in Vietnam," he casually replies. There is a brief silence. She then responds, "My only son, Rene, was killed in the Vietnam War. He was twenty. He was a medic and had only been in Vietnam for two weeks. He was killed trying to care for a wounded soldier. His death was such a waste." Tears fill her eyes. "My son was born on the same day as Prince Charles of England, and whenever I see the prince, I think, this is the age Rene would be. Rene died thirty years ago. He would now be in his fifties, but I can only see him as twenty years old."

We go back to our room in the Kanuga lodge. I have ridden in its slow but steady elevator so many times. Today I see the plaque on the elevator wall. *"This elevator given in memory of Reginald Hudson Bedell, RAF bomber pilot, killed in action December 19, 1942. Born February 13, 1920. Given in memory by his mother, Edna Woods Buist."* Reginald was twenty-two. If he were alive today, he would be eighty-five, a year older than Bea. But to Edna Woods Buist and to all of us who ride the elevator at Kanuga, her son, Reginald, will always be twenty-two. As I reach my floor, the elevator doors open. Suddenly I feel as if I am walking out of a time capsule into a world that has changed very little. I look back to see the elevator doors slowly close behind me.

Heard on *Tales from the South*

INTERPRETING ORDINATION

Ordination of Sam Loudenslager to the Diaconate
Trinity Cathedral • November 23,2002

Barbara Brown Taylor describes ordination, like baptism, as the celebration of a demotion.[1] Unlike sorority initiations or Eagle Scout ceremonies, it is a rite in which we step down, not up. It is a ritual in which we are made the servants of all, and it seems to me that there is rich irony, Sam, in your lining up to do this kind of work. Would any one you know answer a classified ad that said, "Menial labor, long hours, high expectations, no pay?" And yet here you are, Sam.

I am going to ask each of you to turn to page 534 of the order of service at The Examination in the Book of Common Prayer (p. 534).

Sam, in a few minutes, you will stand before Bishop Maze and he will publicly ask you these questions which I know you have read almost daily since you have been in deacon formation. I ask you to ponder them one more time.

"God now calls you to a special ministry of servanthood directly under your bishop."

I sent several pages I had written about servant ministry to my mentor, Rob Seifert, a deacon in California who teaches at the College of Preachers. He red inked most of it and wrote this in the margin in bold letters. "Servant ministry has nothing to do with being 'subservient,' and everything to do with leadership. 'Servant Ministry' is a 'style' of leadership, not a 'list' of things a 'servant Minister' does. Ministry (episcopal, priestly, or diaconal) is always and everywhere leadership and how Jesus wants us to conduct ourselves in its implementation. If we can keep that in mind a whole lot of the nonsense people want to attribute to diaconal ministry will simply fade away."

That means you are to lead people into vision, literally better vision. Popularly your role has been described as the eyes and ears of the bishop. You are called to be a cataract surgeon, removing the scales that blind people from what is going on around them. Sometimes you will be an ear physician, recommending hearing aids when people are deaf to the cry of their neighbor.

"Will you do your best to pattern your life in accordance with the teachings of Christ? Will you be guided by the pastoral direction and leadership of your bishop?"

What a mouthful! The crosier or shepherd's crook is a symbol our bishop carries which is a sign of his office, his symbol that he seeks guidance from the Good Shepherd. Ever since my first trip to England I have been fascinated with sheep and shepherds. This spring my husband, Madge Brown, Merry Helen and I pilgrimaged through England and Scotland from Lindsfarne to Iona. As always the countryside was covered with thousands of sheep on beautiful rolling hillsides. Only once, however, did we see a real shepherd. He did not wear sandals or an animal coat. He was tall and sleek and wore black boots and a long black coat and carried a tall stick. His gait was long and his deliberate pace was like a drum major leading a parade. I have never seen anyone walk with such strength and power. All of the flock were traveling beside him . . . except of course for one lone sheep that had just gone astray.

The shepherd immediately looked at his Border Collie beside him, lifted his staff and pointed to the stray sheep. His faithful dog without hesitating ran out after that lost sheep. With clock like precision, he herded him back to the flock. It was a show stopping sight.

We are here today because we have experienced the safety of living with the flock where we feel as close to the Good Shepherd as possible. That is what our church, our liturgy means for many of us, a safe place walking, sitting, eating close to the master. Being a Border Collie means staying with the flock you so love but also being obedient to the call, following our Lord's direction to be a guide back to his presence.

Being a Border Collie means you have to go out from the flock in order to be a directive for the journey back to safety. Being a Border Collie means leaving the safety of the beaten path. But we are always safe as long as we can hear our master's voice or see his gaze or glimpse his staff. And then there is that unbelievable joy of walking beside him as we return to the flock.

Sam, in a few minutes, our representative of the Good Shepherd is going to pray that you officially become a Border Collie . . . staying with the fold as a leader of the liturgy , but also spending time in places off the path to bring his flock home. You will spend time with the "gathered," but your major work will be in the borderlands with the "scattered."

"As a deacon in the Church, you are to study the Holy Scriptures, to seek nourishment from them, and to model your life upon them."

Today in Acts we heard about the shooting star ministry of Stephen, the first deacon of the church and first martyr, who went down in history for being the first ordinary Christian to follow his good shepherd to the slaughter. This is perhaps what we most fear will happen when we see the shepherd's crosier raised. Stephen was not one of the Twelve. He was not even a candidate to replace Judas when that slot came open. Matthias got the job. As far as we can tell, he was not anyone's idea of headline material. He was simply a good faithful man who could be trusted to distribute food to those who were hungry without putting more on one person's plate than another's. Barbara Brown Taylor[2] thinks that if Stephen had been a better deacon he might not have ended up a martyr as well. In those days, deacons were meant to be seen and not heard. They were supposed to wait tables and not preach. The disciples were the ones who were to devote themselves to the ministry of the word. Stephen's ministry shows us that the diaconate was in "transition" from the get go. For making sack lunches for the widows of Jerusalem turned out to be the least of Stephen's gifts. Once he had hands laid on his head and he was called by name, (just as will be soon done to you, Sam,) all the grace and power that poured into him spilled over as signs and wonders. Luke does not give a lot of details. Maybe Stephen did try to keep a low profile. Maybe he was just handing someone her lunch one day when he healed her by mistake. Maybe he only meant to stir the soup, not the spirit, but the spirit lit on him. It lit him up so that some from the synagogue of the Freedmen could not take their eyes off him until he had seen his last.

There is one difference between you, Sam, and Stephen, and that is that Stephen did not have a bishop to guide him. So maybe the job of our bishop is to keep deacons like us from being in the red and being martyrs . . . or if they do become martyrs that it be for a very good cause!

"At all times, your life and teaching are to show Christ's people that in serving the helpless they are serving Christ himself."

Sam, do you remember where you were the night of April 4, 1968? I know you were living in Memphis and I believe you were about 13. My husband and I were also in Memphis in medical school getting ready to graduate. This was the night that Martin Luther King was assassinated outside of the Loraine Motel in that city. The next day Memphis became a police state. What would be your response today to such violence? Thirty years ago a large group of clergy in (300) decided to respond to this horrendous act by marching to the office of the mayor, Henry Loeb. The clergy gathered at St. Mary's Episcopal Cathedral.[3] At the last moment, the Dean, William Dimmick, who later became the bishop of Michigan, went into the Cathedral and took the cross from the high altar. Holding it high above him (he was a rather short man), he led the march down Poplar Avenue toward City Hall. The air was electric. Down the streets they marched. There were many words spoken that day. One Methodist minister still speaks about one sentence, one turn of phrase that he will never forget. As the clergy were marching down Poplar Avenue, up ahead, he saw an elderly woman sitting on her front porch. As the procession approached her, she stood up and screamed, "GET THAT CROSS BACK IN THE CHURCH WHERE IT BELONGS!" Sam, today this is the ministry you have chosen. Like another clergy from Memphis, today you are called to carry the cross outside of the walls of this cathedral and lead a band of people with you. Our bishop will be asking you to carry that cross out onto Spring Street where it belongs!

You now are traveling with an international passport with dual citizenship, with residences in the church and in the world. You are called to be that bridge between the widening moats, which has been built to separate the church from the world. Sometimes the distance will be so wide, there will be no possibility of a bridge and you will find yourself in a rowboat trying to lead commuters, paddling across as best you can. There is one way, however, I would definitely not try to bridge the gap: that is attempting to walk the water.

"Will you in all things seek not your glory but the glory of the Lord Christ?"

Sam, you already know that you are not volunteering for a life of holy order, but instead a life guiding and mentoring foot washers. Your tools[1] will be a bunch of wet towels, muddy water, and a chronic shortage of soap.

People will always be glad to see you, but never forget that they come to find Jesus.

It is entirely possible that some of your proudest accomplishments will be embarrassing to God, and some of your most dismal failures will please God very much. There is simply no way of telling since our wisdom is so different from God's wisdom.

Sam, as you leave this place and travel from the Broadway exit:

May the Good Shepherd bless you with discomfort at easy answers,
   half-truth and
superficial relationships so that
You will live deep in his heart.
And may the Spirit bless you with enough foolishness
To think you can make a difference in the world,
so that you will do the things
Which others say can never be done.
  ... and Remember that the power behind you is much greater than the
  task in front of you. ... [4]

1. Barbara Brown Taylor, *God in Pain,* p. 45, 48, 136.
2. Barbara Brown Taylor, "Blood of the Martyrs," *Home by Another Way,* pp. 124–128.
3. Katherine Moorehead, "Stepping out of the Tent," *Preaching Through the Year of Mark,* eds. Roger Alling and David J. Schlafer, p. 75.
4. Interfaith Council for Peace and Justice, Ann Arbor, Michigan.

Ordination of Emily Bost to the Diaconate

Jeremiah 1:4–9, 2 Corinthians 4:1–6, Luke 22: 24–27

Trinity Cathedral • December 16, 2006,

"What we preach is not ourselves, but Christ Jesus as Lord and ourselves as your servants." We are the body of Christ. Where is the deacon in the body of Christ?

Luke gives us our best-known description of a deacon, a leader who serves, a servant leader. Emily, I know you have prepared for the diaconate by attending the servant leadership school in Greensboro. Sam, Merry Helen, and Joyce have brought this program back to Arkansas. My vision is that all of us in diaconal ministry or any who think they may be called to ministry should be a part of this program. Servant leaders are the hands and heart of Christ.

Our reading from Jeremiah is a reminder of another description of the deacon, the deacon's voice being the voice of a prophet. Prophets tells us about God's vast love, and then teach, encourage, and empower us to respond to that love by correcting the social injustice in this world. Prophets have a passion for social justice and for God (not just knowledge of God, but a relationship with God). Without passion and love of God in our voice, we are a noisy gong. Prophets must be intoxicated with God. Barbara Brown Taylor has written a book, *Leaving Church,* about what happens when our ministry becomes so overwhelming that we lose that spiritual connection. Her only way back to that passion, her Sabbath was to leave her ministry in the church. She is an icon of how absolutely essential and difficult it is to keep a rule of life, a Sabbath if we want to be a prophet, a deacon who speaks the prophetic voice of Christ.

Another frequent description of the deacon is that of a bridge, someone connecting the church to the world and the world to the church. Our new presiding bishop, Katharine, describes the deacon as a construction foreman[1] building new bridges in the desert between the old and the new. Her icon for this construction supervisor is John the Baptist, the prophet of the New Testament. How very appropriate, Emily, that your ordination is framed by Advent 2 and Advent 3, both Sundays in our lectionary where John the Baptist comes glaring at us in full force.

He rearranges the walls around Israel to create a new opening into the hearts of people. He is both a demolition expert and a foundation builder. All that business about "repenting" is asking the people of Israel to tear down the false front they have been hiding behind, and then use the waters in the Jordan to make a stronger concrete foundation. But after the foundation is built, John gets out of the way. For then his cousin comes along and builds on the foundation that John has pains takingly started. But the building doesn't end up being the stone fortress Israel wants. For walls, this home has the open air. There is room for everyone imaginable to come in. The food is simple, but there is enough to spare.

Today's John, the deacon prophet, is really an expert remodeler. She is in overalls instead of animal skins. She is not the sort of architect who spends all day in the office. She gets out in the field, puts on a hard hat, and mucks around in the foundation hole. The deacon, the construction supervisor is the planner, the mind of Christ.

Emily, we are also here to remind you, "always wear your hard hat." It is your protection. The hard hat represents the covering of your head with the mind of Christ. Without the mind of Christ, your hard hat, your body will be in danger of grave injury. Your heart will eventually harden, and you will no longer be sharing the love of God that brought you to this ministry.

And so, dear friends, we are here today to give thanks for John and his younger cousin and to name, Emily, another construction supervisor to help build more foundations and lead others to tear down and build new foundations. Emily, you already know much about remodeling and building bridges. You are being ordained to continue to build bridges between your community, your church and the battered women's shelter. You are building bridges and leading others to the Mississippi gulf coast still ravaged from Katrina. You will learn even more about how to dismantle exclusive weak and dangerous bridges built on hierarchy and prejudice and build new ones in their places.

Emily, we are asking you to stand with us and lead us to the edge, between two cultures, where you can help us build broader, more inclusive bridges. Sometimes it is lonely, but the scenery is gorgeous. As you move back and forth you can tell us about the people who haven't gotten close to the bridge from either side. Your special concern will not only be people who have not yet found the bridge, but also people who have been knocked off the bridge, both out and in the church. Your job is to find them and remind us to look for them. Sometimes, as Pogo says, they may be us. The architecture of these bridges is holy, mysterious. Your job, Emily, is to hold up God's blueprint, mobilize the construction crew, tell the people on each end of the project what the people on the other end are doing.

And when we resist, you may even sometimes have to tell us, "Repent, turn around," just like your role model.

Emily, your work should never be carried out alone. This single person ministry that is all on one person's shoulders is what Parker Palmer calls functional atheism.[2] Bridges are not built by individuals. They need enormous crews and trained crews. Sometimes, Emily, a great deal of your time may be training a crew. But you have many tools. You have the tools of deacon formation, EFM, Community of Hope, servant leadership to train others for ministry.

For years we have been watching the building of bridges on I 40. Some are still not finished. Often this will happen to you. You may start a bridge from one side, but the time to build the other end has not yet come. John's ministry is like that. He preaches and baptizes and then goes to prison and to his death without seeing the whole bridge finished. He has an inkling of what might be coming, some kind of blueprint, but he never gets to see the Easter Bridge. The work of the deacon is often like that. It calls for faithfulness, not waiting around for the end results.

The work of the deacon is indeed so much like John's: stay intimately connected to God, listen for the truth, speak your truth as articulately as you can, and then get out of the way when people start to listen. That's pretty counter cultural, but that is what living on the edge, servant leadership is all about, "learning how to stand in the face of others without having to take up all the space." Like John, when the time is right you will be asked to get out of the way so that someone else's message can be heard.

In *Indiana Jones and the Last Crusade,* the hero is told he will have to cross a great chasm to reach his goal. There is no obvious bridge. All he can see is empty space. But he has been told that a bridge of light will appear once he commits himself and steps out over that void. He finally rustles up his courage and steps out; the bridge materializes before him. Emily, your job is to encourage all of us to share our visions and step out and be willing to trust God's vision for that bridge.

But in another sense, this day is not just about you, Emily, even though you are being given the speaking role of John the Baptist. This day is about each of us, and the kinds of bridges we are going to build. We all are called to build bridges because that is what we are asked to do at our baptism. Emily, you are being called to remind us of that. Today we are being given a new foreman, and we are being asked to let her lead us.

Emily, time to get the body of Christ, your crew moving. Time to hold up the blueprint, point to the design of Christ, to see Christ in every human being. The call is out. The whistle is blowing, the drums are beating, the bells are ringing. It's your watch now. The bridge is a-building.

1. Katharine Jefferts Schori, "Bridge Building/Circle Widening," *Preaching Through Holy Days and Holidays, Sermons that Work XI,* pp. 51–53.
2. Parker Palmer, *Let Your Life Speak,* p.88.

INTERPRETING RECOVERY

Recovery Sunday

Matthew 18:12–14
Calvary Episcopal Church, Memphis, Tenn. • October 8, 2006

"It is not the will of your Father in heaven that one of these little ones should be lost."

Chances are that 10% of the people in this room are alcoholics. One in five of all households in this church experience alcoholism[1]. It is the number two killer in this country behind cancer. For centuries alcoholism has been seen as a moral problem.[2] Finally in 1956 the American Medical Association (AMA) recognized alcoholism as a disease.[2] It is a progressive, hereditary disease, a physical addiction.[2] Some chemical imbalance in the alcoholic does not trigger the normal feed back mechanism that most people have to stop drinking when they reach some limit. The treatment is abstinence. The major premise of Alcoholics Anonymous (AA), a 12-step program, probably the most successful treatment for the disease, is seeking help from a power greater than yourself. The treatment is a spiritual one. You at Calvary should be especially interested to know that most of the teachings of AA came from an Episcopal priest, Sam Shoemaker, rector of another Calvary Episcopal Church in New York City.

I would like to share with you one alcoholic's story. She has given me permission to do so. She had her first drink when she was a junior in college. She only drank on weekends at her aunt's home at the cocktail hour. She went through medical school and residency and perhaps had one drink a day, for relaxation from a hectic schedule. Then with her first job, working 10 to 12 hour days, she developed a pattern where alcohol became a central part of her life. She would come home from the hospital; have two drinks before dinner, two during dinner, and two after dinner. Then she would go to sleep to awaken the next day to the same routine. She attained notable success in her profession, but the people she was not there for were her husband and three children. When they would ask questions about homework at night, she would just smile at them. She was a quiet alcoholic. She knew if she spoke, people would know she had had too much to drink, so she became quieter and quieter. People began to see her as a very spiritual person. The lesson here is, if you want people to think you are spiritual, just don't say much. She was filled with the spirit, but a very different spirit. She served on vestries, keeping her mask of quietness, the perfect vestry member. She was very careful not to let her drinking interfere with her work. She never drank when she was on call.

She started going to a therapist for "difficulties accepting life on life's terms." The therapist wondered if she might benefit from a 12-step group. No, AA was not for her. That was for people who lived under the bridge and old men who smoked a lot. One work night she had a meeting at her house for other physicians in her department. She broke her work rule, and had too much to drink. The next morning she had a terrible hangover. She went to the hospital, and it was one of those days where you have to be on your toes every second. She prayed that if God would keep her from not hurting any one that day, she would stop drinking. She can't remember if she hurt any of her patients that day, but the next night she was at her favorite restaurant drinking champagne at a party honoring one of her partners. She was to get up and make a speech, but she just sat there, smiling at everyone. She knew if she said anything, they would know she had had too much to drink. Somehow this night became a moment of clarity. She knew she was crossing the line from being a functional alcoholic. She knew she was powerless over alcohol and that her life was becoming unmanageable. Soon down the road, her drinking was going to interfere with her work. Many alcoholic stories are like this. Work seems to be the last part of their life to be compromised. She went back to her therapist who connected her to a member of AA. This woman had graduated from high school. Our friend had many degrees, but this woman knew more about living. This sponsor kept her sober taking her to meetings almost every day. Our friend soon learned that the answer to sobriety was a spiritual life, taking the second and third steps of AA, knowing that a power greater than herself could restore her to sanity and turning her life and her will over to God. When she heard this, she thought it was hopeless. She was a spiritual person; everyone knew that. She attended church regularly, wrote for religious magazines, held retreats. What she learned in AA, however, was something that she had been taught in church, but somehow never got. You have seen these bumper stickers, "God is my copilot." That was true for her, but she was the pilot. Her relationship to God was that God was there to help her get done what she wanted to accomplish. She had not turned her life over to God for God's purposes. She learned to live the Serenity Prayer, praying for the knowledge to know what she could do something about in her life and accepting what she could not do something about. She went to AA meetings almost every day for 10 years, learning that staying sober was staying in community with a group of people also trying to live their life as honestly as possible with God at the center. Living the 12 steps meant taking an inventory every day, making amends to those she had harmed, taking off the mask that she was the perfect person. She made amends to her family, for those were the ones she had most harmed. Two of her children were in college; one was in high school. She had not been there for them at crucial times. Was it hopeless? She talks about making amends to one of her sons, in a restaurant (as you can see, she likes to eat). She told him she wanted to change. His response is branded on her heart, "Mom, it is never too late to change." Soon all of her children went away to school. Then all of them returned back home. Friends told her how awful it was that her children were back home. But she loved it. God had given her another chance to relate to her children and be a mom. She has now been sober for 15 years, 10 months and 20 days. She still goes to two AA meetings a week. She has five grandchildren with whom she spends much of her time. We often talk about what her life would be like if she had not gone to AA. She most probably would be dead. She would have missed the unbelievable joy of being a grandmother, of becoming an ordained deacon in the Episcopal Church, and being here to be with you today to share my story of how a power greater than myself working in community saved my life. And I am here this morning to tell you that the same can happen to you.

"It is not the will of your Father in heaven that one of these little ones should be lost."

1. Childress J. F., and Macquarrie, John, *The Westminster Dictionary of Christian Ethics,* p. 18, The Westminster Press, 1967.
2. Milam, James R., and Ketcham, Katherine, *Under the Influence,* pp. 8, 146, 36, 39–42. Bantam, 1988.

ABOUT THE AUTHOR

Photograph by Sean Moorman.

DR. JOANNA SEIBERT is a professor of radiology and pediatrics at Arkansas Children's Hospital and the University of Arkansas Medical Sciences. She has been an ordained deacon in the Episcopal Diocese of Arkansas for fourteen years. She has served as a deacon at St. Margaret's Episcopal Church, Trinity Cathedral Little Rock, and now is assigned to St. Luke's North Little Rock. Her most recent book is *Taste and See*, written with her daughter Joanna ES Campbell about seeing God's presence in difficult situations and food is always present! Previous books include *The Call of the Psalms, a spiritual companion for busy people* and *The Call of the Psalms, a spiritual companion for people in recovery*. The two books are stories in response to the 150 psalms. She also has written a book, *Healing Presence*, about visiting the sick and dying and grieving. She also edited a book of meditations on the Eucharistic readings, *Surrounded by a Cloud of Witnesses*, has been a writer for *Forward, Day by Day,* and has been a frequent contributor to the *Living Church* and the *Anglican Digest*. She and her husband, Robert, for eight years were Arkansas' representatives to the National Cathedral in Washington. She is a facilitator for the Community of Hope, Walking the Mourner's Path, and involved in Crisis Response Team in the Diocese of Arkansas. She previously has been on the board of the National Recovery Ministries of the Episcopal Church and the Camp Mitchell board. She was named one of three "women of distinction" in Arkansas in 1992 and has been named one of the top 100 women in Arkansas by *Arkansas Business* for several years as well as being on the list of outstanding doctors in the country for many years. She is a former president and chairman of the board of the Society for Pediatric Radiology. Arkansas Children's Hospital annually gives an award to the physician at the hospital who embodies teamwork in his or her practice. The award is named the Robert and Joanna Seibert award.

Joanna and her husband Robert have three grown children and six grandchildren and have lived in Little Rock for almost forty years.

Druck:
Canon Deutschland Business Services GmbH
im Auftrag der KNV-Gruppe
Ferdinand-Jühlke-Str. 7
99095 Erfurt